'A much needed rethinking of the variability of neoliberal education projects and neoliberal subjectivities in different national contexts.'

Steven Ward, *Professor of Sociology, Western Connecticut State University, USA*

'Considering how neoliberalism works and what it does to education in specific national and local settings has been a key concern of critical sociology of education for some time. This collection of essays by Reimers, Martinson and colleagues extends this work by engaging in the crucial task of detailing the political subjects that are called up and curtailed in these conditions. Understanding the possibilities for responding to neoliberal tendencies in education remains a pressing task for scholars, activists and educators and so this collection provides important resources for thinking about and doing politics in and against neoliberal education.'

Deborah Youdell, *Professor of Sociology of Education, University of Birmingham, UK*

Education and Political Subjectivities in Neoliberal Times and Places

Education and Political Subjectivities in Neoliberal Times and Places investigates the conditions and possibilities for political subjectivities to emerge in international educational contexts, where neoliberal norms are repeated, performed and transformed. Through demonstrating the possibility of political subjectivities, this book argues that neoliberalism should neither be considered post-political nor a natural law by which educational practises have to abide.

This book considers how political subjectivities are made possible in education in spite of dominant neoliberal norms. The chapters address key theoretical discussions surrounding these different, sometimes contradicting, norms and their relationship to education, economy and politics. This innovative approach considers diverse educational and political initiatives in the wake of new public management, postcolonial perspectives on neoliberal education, and educational practises and critical possibilities. The book advocates understanding and enacting democracy as an experiment, based on the conception that democracy is constantly constructed and constitutes a transformative process in society in general as well as in education.

This book advances the argument that there is still room for political subjectivity in spite of the dominance of neoliberal educational governance. It will appeal to researchers, academics and postgraduate students in the fields of higher education, education policy and politics, sociology of education and comparative and international education, as well as those interested in neoliberalism, new public management and inequality.

Eva Reimers is Professor of Educational Practise at Linköping University, Sweden.

Lena Martinsson is Professor of Gender Studies in the Department for Cultural Sciences, University of Gothenburg, Sweden.

Routledge Research in Education Policy and Politics

For a full list of titles in this series, please visit www.routledge.com

The Routledge Research in Education Policy and Politics series aims to enhance our understanding of key challenges and facilitate on-going academic debate within the influential and growing field of Education Policy and Politics.

Books in the series include:

Educational Binds of Poverty
The lives of school children
Ceri Brown

Pedagogy, Praxis and Purpose in Education
C. M. Mulcahy, D. E. Mulcahy, and D. G. Mulcahy

Creativity and Democracy in Education
Practices and politics of education through the arts
Jeff Adams and Allan Owens

Teachers' Unions and Education Reform in Comparative Contexts
Lindsay M. Whorton

Political and Social Influences on the Education of Children
Research from Bosnia to Herzegovina
Gwyneth Owen-Jackson

The Strong State and Curriculum Reform
Assessing the Politics and Possibilities of Educational Change in Asia
Leonel Lim and Michael W. Apple

Modernising School Governance
Corporate planning and expert handling in state education
Andrew Wilkins

UNESCO Without Borders
Educational campaigns for international understanding
Edited by Aigul Kulnazarova and Christian Ydesen

Education and Political Subjectivities in Neoliberal Times and Places
Emergences of norms and possibilities
Edited by Eva Reimers and Lena Martinsson

Education and Political Subjectivities in Neoliberal Times and Places

Emergences of norms and possibilities

Edited by Eva Reimers and Lena Martinsson

LONDON AND NEW YORK

First published 2017
by Routledge
2 Park Square, Milton Park, Abingdon, Oxon OX14 4RN

and by Routledge
711 Third Avenue, New York, NY 10017

First issued in paperback 2018

Routledge is an imprint of the Taylor & Francis Group, an informa business

© 2017 selection and editorial matter, Eva Reimers and Lena Martinsson; individual chapters, the contributors

The right of the editors to be identified as the authors of the editorial material, and of the authors for their individual chapters, has been asserted in accordance with sections 77 and 78 of the Copyright, Designs and Patents Act 1988.

All rights reserved. No part of this book may be reprinted or reproduced or utilised in any form or by any electronic, mechanical, or other means, now known or hereafter invented, including photocopying and recording, or in any information storage or retrieval system, without permission in writing from the publishers.

Trademark notice: Product or corporate names may be trademarks or registered trademarks, and are used only for identification and explanation without intent to infringe.

British Library Cataloguing in Publication Data
A catalogue record for this book is available from the British Library

Library of Congress Cataloging-in-Publication Data
Names: Reimers, Eva, editor. | Martinsson, Lena, editor.
Title: Education and political subjectivities in neoliberal times and places : emergences of norms and possibilities / edited by Eva Reimers and Lena Martinsson.
Description: New York, NY : Routledge, 2016. | Includes bibliographical references.
Identifiers: LCCN 2016021544 | ISBN 9781138962880 (hardcover) | ISBN 9781315659138 (electronic)
Subjects: LCSH: Education—Political aspects. | Education and globalization. | Neoliberalism.
Classification: LCC LC71 .E287 2016 | DDC 379—dc23
LC record available at https://lccn.loc.gov/2016021544

ISBN 13: 978-1-138-60204-5 (pbk)
ISBN 13: 978-1-138-96288-0 (hbk)

Typeset in Galliard
by Apex CoVantage, LLC

Contents

	Acknowledgements	ix
	Notes on editors	xi
	Notes on contributors	xiii
1	**Introduction: Making trouble with neoliberalism, education and political subjectivity** LENA MARTINSSON AND EVA REIMERS	1
2	**Politics, subjectivity and education in neoliberal times: an interview with Gert Biesta** GERT BIESTA, LENA MARTINSSON AND EVA REIMERS	14
3	**Messy norms and the desire for education** LENA MARTINSSON	31
4	**Competition, accountability and performativity: exploring schizoid neo-liberal 'equality objectives' in a UK primary school** JOS HARVEY AND JESSICA RINGROSE	49
5	**Towards de-cold-war politics: nationalism, democracy and new politics of/for education in Japan** KEITA TAKAYAMA	68
6	**Post-political governing of welfare state education in Sweden** RITA FOSS LINDBLAD AND SVERKER LINDBLAD	86
7	**Why education? Economic and political subjectivities in public discourses on education** EVA REIMERS	101

viii *Contents*

8 **Political subjectivity, political struggle and political education in times of precarisation**   118

EVA REIMERS AND LENA MARTINSSON

9 **Political subjectivity and the experiment of democracy: a conclusion**   130

LENA MARTINSSON AND EVA REIMERS

Index   135

Acknowledgements

The idea for this book took shape following a symposium at AERA 2013. The theme for the symposium was 'Neoliberal Education and Political Subjectivity'. The symposium as well as some of the research serving as the foundation for this book was funded by the Swedish Research Council as part of the projects 'Class in Neoliberal Education Discourses' and 'Dreaming Change: Women and the Creation of Civil Societies in Europe, Asia, and Latin America'.

Notes on editors

Eva Reimers is Professor of Educational Practise at Linköping University, Sweden. Her research focus is on norms and diversity in education. Together with Lena Martinsson, she has edited several books, including *School in Norms [Skola i normer]* (Martinsson and Reimers 2008), reprinted several times, with a new extended edition published in 2014; Norm-Struggles (Martinsson and Reimers 2010); and *Norms at Work* (2007). Her recent publications include the article 'Discourses of Education and Constitutions of Class: Public Discourses on Education in Swedish PBS Television', *Discourse: Studies in the Cultural Politics of Education* 35(4).

Lena Martinsson is Professor in Gender Studies in the Department for Cultural Sciences, University of Gothenburg, Sweden. Her research interests focus on intersectional, queer and postcolonial studies in relation to norms on gender equality and diversity. She has edited several books, including *Challenging the Myth of Gender Equality in Sweden* (2016), together with Gabriele Griffin and Katarina Giritli Nygren; *Norm-Struggles* (Martinsson and Reimers 2010); *School in Norms [Skola i normer]* (Martinsson and Reimers 2008, reprinted several times, with a new extended edition published in 2014); and *Norms at Work* (Martinsson, Reingarde and Reimers 2007).

References

Martinsson, L., Reimers, E., Reingarde, J. (Eds.) (2007). *Norms at Work. Challenging Homophobia and Heteronormativity.* Stockholm: Under Ytan.

Martinsson, L. and Reimers, E. (2007). Towards a disharmonious pluralism: Discourse analysis of official discourses about social diversity. In A. Lin (Ed.). *Problematizing identity: Everyday struggles in language, culture and education* (pp. 51–65). London & New York: Lawrence Erlbaum.

Martinsson, L. and Reimers, E. (Eds.) (2008). (1st edition). *Skola i normer* [A school (schooling) in norms]. Malmö: Gleerups.

Martinsson, L. and Reimers, E. (Eds.) (2014). (2nd edition). *Skola i normer* [A school (schooling) in norms]. Malmö: Gleerups.

Martinsson, L. and Reimers, E. (2010). *Norm-Struggles. Sexualities in Contentions.* Newcastle Upon Tyne: Cambridge Scholars Publishing.

Reimers, E. (2014). Discourses of Education and Constitutions of Class – Public Discourses on Education in Swedish PBS Television. In *Discourse: Studies in the Cultural Politics of Education*, 35(4), 540–553.

Notes on contributors

Gert Biesta is a Professor of Educational Theory and Policy at the University of Luxembourg. He writes about the theory and philosophy of education; the theory of educational research; teaching, learning, curriculum and pedagogy; teacher education; and education policy. Biesta conducts research on such topics as lifelong learning, citizenship, democratic education, curriculum and vocational education.

Rita Foss Lindblad is a Professor of Educational Practise at the University of Borås. With a point of departure in the theory of science, her research interests are relations between the science of education and politics, lifelong learning, professionalisation and processes of educational restructuring.

Jos Harvey is an Early Years educator currently teaching at a large nursery in East London. Jos completed a PGCE specialising in schools in challenging circumstances and has subsequently worked in a variety of settings in areas with high levels of deprivation. Jos recently completed an MA in Social Justice and Education at the UCL Institute of Education, London.

Sverker Lindblad is a Professor of Education at the University of Gothenburg. His research involves the formation of educational systems and processes and how these are linked to various aspects and tendencies in society. Political aspects of educational phenomena are of special interest to him. Lindblad consequently does research in the areas of teaching and in curriculum theory, education policy analysis and school organisation and processes.

Jessica Ringrose is a Professor of Sociology of Gender and Education at the UCL Institute of Education, London. She teaches in the areas of social justice, gender, sexuality and feminist qualitative research. She is currently researching digital feminist activism, with a particular focus on teen feminist and gender and sexuality activism in and around school.

Keita Takayama is an Associate Professor at the School of Education, University of New England. He teaches and researches in the area of the sociology of education/comparative education. Much of his research work concerns the globalisation of education policymaking, with a particular focus on the intersection between the OECD's education work and national policymaking.

1 Introduction

Making trouble with neoliberalism, education and political subjectivity

Lena Martinsson and Eva Reimers

> 'With guns you can kill terrorists, with education you can kill terrorism'.
>
> Malala Yousafzai

The aspirations put into education as a tool to shape the future are numerous. The Nobel laureate Malala Yousafzai is renowned for the way she puts forward education for all children as an antidote to ignorance and violence and as a powerful tool to create a better future. In this, she is not alone. Education is repeatedly presented as a means both to build peace (UNESCO 2016) as well as to achieve economic growth (OECD 2016). It is also represented as a way to achieve equality and to form a sustainable future. The aspirations for education are voiced by the subaltern people as well as those in the affluent and dominant economies. Opinions about how education practices should be performed and governed are formulated from all different political ideologies, from right-wing nationalists to left-wing radicals. This ubiquitous interest in education makes it clear that education is political, formed by politics, used by politics and producing politics.

The above becomes apparent in how education is often entangled with neoliberalism. In different parts of the world, neoliberalism works as a normative transnational force with the aim of creating societal change, and one of its targets is education. Although we take a critical position in regard to the neoliberal norm in education, the objective of this book is to simultaneously point to or follow what emerges from iterations of the neoliberal norm in education in different places and practises, where multiple norms both counteract and act together with the neoliberal norms. We will scrutinise the role not only of neoliberal norm repetitions, which has been done extensively in earlier research (see, e.g., Ball 2012, 2013; Buras and Apple 2005; Connell 2013; Davies and Bansel 2007; Meyer and Benavot 2013), but also of contradictions, interruptions and messiness in order to understand the relationship between education and (im)possible political subjectivities in a neoliberal time (cf. Biesta 2014; Mouffe 2013; Butler 2004; Deleuze and Guattari 1988; Youdell 2006, 2011).

The individual chapters investigate the emergence of educational and neoliberal norms in a variety of situations and places in different parts of the world. One ambition is consequently to challenge the story of neoliberalism as a story of unavoidable development where the West leads 'the rest' (Rofel 2007). Another

2   Lena Martinsson and Eva Reimers

ambition is to scrutinise how the neoliberal normativity is co-materialised with local as well as transnational norms that have an impact both on the ongoing multiple and diversified emergence of neoliberalism and on how places and territories emerge (Massey 2005).

In this book, the term 'neoliberalism' in education refers to some significant traits that are observable in different educational systems and settings. In dealing with neoliberalism in education, we refer to education primarily as formal education, in the form of compulsory education or as initiatives to promote and instigate elementary education. In the book, there are studies of how neoliberalism intersect with education in primary school, in a rural feudal village, in national curricula and in transnational education policy, as well as a chapter on the philosophy of education. These different spaces for performances of neoliberal education point to the messiness and contingency of neoliberalism and education. Despite this messiness, there are observable traits of neoliberalism in education. These are based on the presumption that the market will solve salient problems (Harvey 2006). Although neoliberalism in education is neither unequivocal nor uncontested, it is present and often manifested in assertions of the values of competition, school choice reforms, market principle governance and differing practises of audit cultures (Lindblad and Popkewitz 2004). This has implications not only for practises of education, but also for how to make sense of education and for how subjectivities – as teachers, students and citizens – are made possible in education (Ball 2013). In this book, we address two recurrent phenomena in relation to neoliberal educational practises. Both of them problematise how the neoliberal norm, striving for cohesion and non-political situations through neoliberal hegemony, plays a part in differentiations as well as the emergence of unpredictable subjectivities. The first phenomenon is the limitation of the notion of citizenship education (as it appears in neoliberal policy documents) to participation in democratic processes. This enforces cohesion – the marketisation of education is supposed to benefit everyone – yet it does not develop critical or analytical thinking or practises, nor does it encourage the emergence of political alternatives (cf. Mouffe 2005; Brown 2015; Spivak 2008). It does not create possibilities for political subjectification (Biesta 2014). However, subjectivities emerge not only within norms but also in the entangled crossroads between them (cf. Ball 2013, p. 16). Thus, it is not possible to predict what subjectivity and concomitant agency will emerge from these messy processes that also involve neoliberalism. A specific interest in this book is therefore how political subjectivities – defined as abilities to recognise political alternatives and conflicts and to imagine changes – are made possible in the crossroads of and the ongoing emergence of norms. The other phenomenon we address is the role played by neoliberal normativity in an ongoing differentialisation and segregation between nations, races and classes. In contrast to the ideology of cohesion, the neoliberal educational reforms have severely deepened the problem of segregation and the significance of class for school achievement in many countries (Apple 2002; Ball 2006; Connell 2013; Swedish National Agency of Education 2009, 2012).

We want to shed some light on possibilities and impediments for political agency in a situation where lots of people find themselves positioned outside

Introduction 3

the political. There is a tension between citizenship and political subjectivity. Citizenship is connected to being a citizen of a nation-state. As a citizen, you are supposed to be recognised and protected by the state. In order to get rights, there must be a community or a nation that give you these rights. In Chapter 2, Biesta discuss two ways of understanding citizenship in the context of citizenship education. The first is primarily connected to belonging, rights and duties, where pupils are expected to be socialised into citizenship. The other is citizenship as subjectification, where pupils are agents within the formation and performance of democracy. Citizenship is thereby not necessarily tantamount to political subjectivity. Citizenship as socialisation is focused on social cohesion, whereas citizenship as subjectivisation is focused on continuously forming a 'better' democracy. In several chapters in this book, we have chosen to use the concept of political subjectivity, not citizenship. This is because this concept makes it possible to study the possibility for political subjectivity to emerge among people who are not recognised by the state, who live in vulnerable or precarious situations or are children.

One presumption that we share with many others is that education can make a difference. In our argumentation, we focus on the unpredictability and messiness of differing educational assemblages (Deleuze and Guattari 1988) in the form of entanglements with world politics, economic interests, norms, practises and materialities. We ask questions about which different subjectivities can emerge in or through these formations. We thereby take issue with a conception of neoliberal educational policies and practises as determinants of a post-political situation, in which neoliberal ideology is made into more or less a natural law by which educational practises and reforms have to abide.

Neoliberal normativity

In our interest in what emerges from iterations of the neoliberal norm in education in different places and practises, it is important to point out that we regard neoliberalism as a transnational norm, not an intentional conspiracy. As a norm, repeated and enacted in multiple places, neoliberalism brings about societal change, not least in the field of education (Brown 2015). Educational practises are thus often both produced by and part of neoliberal normativity.

A premise for this book is a conception of neoliberal norms signified by specific traits that are observable in different educational systems and settings. These traits are based on the presumption that the market will solve problems such as the challenge of maintaining an employable workforce, deficits in the democracy, poor school performance, inequality, lack of economic growth etc. (Ball 2013). Neoliberal ways of solving social problems are characterised by a conception of human subjectivity as individual and rational. By denying the relevance of collective positionings and interests, neoliberal practises turn a blind eye to, or blatantly deny the relevance of, interdependency and collective experiences or interests (Butler 2015). This is why, as Chantal Mouffe claims, neoliberalism fails to grasp the pluralistic nature of the (social) world and the conflicts this entails (Mouffe 2005, p. 10). This is also why neoliberal normativity makes it possible to assume

4   *Lena Martinsson and Eva Reimers*

that the political work for societal change is unnecessary and possible to ignore unless the aim of politics is to further the objectives of the market.

The traits of the neoliberal are neither unequivocal nor uncontested. However, they are present and often manifested in assertions of the value of competition between countries, schools and students, as well as in school choice reforms, New Public Management governance and differing practises of audit cultures (Lindblad and Popkewitz 2004). The description is also often connected to the idea that the welfare state has grown too big and needs to be dismantled (Harvey 2006). In this book, we address these neoliberal traits in education in different regions, contexts and countries such as Pakistan, Japan, Great Britain and Sweden and in multilateral organisations, in order to show how they are situationally reiterated and transformed and with what effects.

A common feature for most previous research on neoliberal repetitions in education is that it regards neoliberal educational practises as hegemonic and identical repetitions regardless of where they are repeated. However, this book highlights that the neoliberal norms in education are part of a plethora of differing and intersecting normative materialities and practises. There are thus both similarities and many differences between how neoliberal norms are reiterated.

The fluidity of places

The individual chapters investigate the emergence of educational and neoliberal norms in different places. Here, places are not understood as stable contexts in which neoliberalism intervenes, nor as explanatory factors, but as assemblages of artefacts, norms, narratives, people and activities. Neither are they understood through a paradigm of development (cf. Massey 2005). This fluid and contingent notion of place is important because it challenges the notion of stable nation states bound to geographical places. It thus facilitates scrutinising how the neoliberal normativity is co-materialised with local as well as transnational norms that have an impact both on the ongoing multiple and diversified emergence of neoliberalism and on how places and territories emerge (Massey 2005). To give an example, the place Sweden as a nation can be understood as an assemblage where stories, politics and materialities are co-materialised with norms that often go beyond the borders of the nation. The norms stabilise understandings of the nation and in that way are performative, and they produce frictions concerning borders and belonging. When neoliberalism, for example, is reiterated in Sweden, with its former social democratic welfare politics that have been of huge importance for how the educational system was once structured, the consequences are different than when neoliberalism is plugged into a nation without a welfare state. This is the case in Chapter 3 in this book, where Martinsson recounts effects of neoliberalism in education in a society without a welfare system. She describes how education as well as neoliberal normativity are plugged into a feudal assemblage, a village with earlier colonial traits, and how the feudal village assemblage as well as the villagers, the place and its inhabitants are transformed in these processes. It is apparent that neoliberalism emerges around the globe in different ways, with different effects, and is consequently also transformed. Thus, the differing performances of the neo-liberal cannot solely be attributed to regional or national political specificities. Keita Takayama's chapter in this book exemplifies how national Japanese educational reforms are part of transnational forces and politics. Takayama understands the Japanese dependency on the US, visible in popular culture as well as politics, people's habits and ideology (cf. Grewal 2005), as reminiscent of the Cold War, which is important for the emergence of national subjectivities and the educational debate and reforms in Japan. He explores how the 'cold-war-era education scholarship' plugged into the rise of neoliberalism in the 1990s, where the binary juxtaposition of private (individual freedom) and state control was reconciled by the neoliberal claims of achieving both individuality and freedom via choice.

Cohesion and precarisation

Based on the above, it becomes apparent that reiterations of neoliberalism never are, nor can they be, unequivocal. There are thus always contradictions and frictions in how educational practises are performed and understood together with the neoliberal. It is therefore not possible to completely predict how education practises will be performed and with what effects.

One contradiction in enunciations of education concerns differentiations emerging from neoliberal practises and policies. Neoliberal ideology is based on the notion that the interests of the market are tantamount to the interests of society. The aim of politics is consequently formulated as creating the best possible conditions for the market (Mouffe 2005; Harvey 2006). In Chapter 2, Gert Biesta asserts that at the same time as neoliberal norms presume social cohesion in terms of consensus regarding the borders, goals and governance of society, the effects of neoliberal policies and practises often increase segregation. The gaps increase between different classed and/or racialised positions between those that are considered valuable and those that, from a neoliberal market perspective, are seen as burdens to society. This is how neoliberal normativity produces an ongoing precarisation, where parts of the population are subjected to increased insecurity (Butler 2015). Consequently, neoliberal practises increase conflicts and antagonism between different positions and collectives.

A central precondition for the precarisation effects of neoliberal normativity is the pivotal position of competition. It is a notion based on the presumption of winners and losers. In order for the economy and society to flourish, some nations, categories, collectives or individuals have to succeed at the expense of others. At the same time, as Jos Harvey and Jessica Ringrose show in Chapter 4, neoliberal normativity is based on the notion of independent and rational individuals, thereby denying effects of discrimination and subordination based on how people are categorised in terms of gender, race, class, functionality, sexuality, religion and age. The precarious positions in which many find themselves is assumed to be an effect of poor choices or laziness, not of power differences or differing prerequisites. The children interviewed in Harvey and Ringrose's chapter recount the limits of assessing inequality and discrimination based solely on

6 *Lena Martinsson and Eva Reimers*

what is possible to measure. These children demonstrated much more complex understandings of how inequality and discrimination worked in the school.

Neoliberal normativity partly conceals its segregational effects by stressing the notion of the benefits of diversity. It thereby becomes possible to see differing identity positions as complementary rather than agonistic and oppositional. An example of this is the frequently used business term 'diversity management', which frames identity positions as complementary talents and perspectives rather than as effects of different conditions and possibilities due to processes of racialisation, gendering norms and ageism (Martinsson and Reimers 2007, 2010). The discourse of diversity thus affirms the idea of cohesion by stressing that difference is not a threat against a cohesive totality: quite the opposite. Diversity strengthens and affirms the idea of a society with common interests for all (citizens). The shared interests in a society dominated by neoliberalism are furthermore considered so given and fundamental that they emerge as non-political. Cohesion, or the notion of cohesion, thereby comes forward as beyond politics, or as non- or post-political (cf. Mouffe 2005). In this book, we challenge this understanding of cohesion as consensus regarding the supremacy of the market. The question of importance for us is instead how it is possible to struggle for a society where processes of precarisation are recognised and problematised in order to create equality.

The contradictions or tensions between cohesion and differentiation have implications for the notion of education that appears in neoliberal citizenship education policy documents. As demonstrated by Eva Reimers in this book, citizenship is here often limited to participation in democratic processes in order to enforce cohesion – the marketisation is supposed to be good for one and all – not to develop critical or analytical thinking or practises or to encourage the emergence of political alternatives (cf. Mouffe 2005; Brown 2015; Spivak 2008), that is, to create conditions for political subjectivity (Biesta et al. 2014).

Political subjectivity emerging in pluralities

As mentioned earlier, in scrutinising the relations between education and political subjectivity in different places, we use a definition of political subjectivity as a feeling and understanding that, firstly, something in the present situation is wrong; secondly, there are alternatives to this situation; and thirdly, I, or we, can bring about difference. In this book there are different, but closely affiliated, conceptions of the necessary conditions for the emergence of political subjectivity. In Chapter 2, rather than using the term 'political subjectivity', Biesta juxtaposes 'subjectification' (of individuals) to describe how pupils and students emerge as political subjects, and the term 'socialisation' to describe how pupils and students emerge as compliant citizens. Drawing on Rancière, Biesta focuses on the concept of democratic politics, which is defined as the interruption of a social order with reference to freedom, equality and solidarity.

A common theme for several authors in this book is the importance of plurality of interests, identities, norms and discourses for political subjectivity to emerge. In Chapter 2, Biesta argues that plurality is not a problem that needs to be solved but something that should be valued. This is because, according to Biesta, plurality is the condition for subjectification, which he describes as 'becoming in plurality'.

Plurality is a concept that is repeated in different ways and in different contexts in the various chapters in the book. We believe it is important to stress that when we speak of plurality in terms of norms and identities, plurality is not solely an asset for development of democracy and political subjectivities. Pluralities of normative materialisations always produce inclusions and exclusions. Some feelings, identities or practises emerge as normative, whereas others are made strange, unintelligible or marginalised. We believe it is important to ask how the plurality of norms plays out in neoliberal educational discourses and policies. In Harvey and Ringrose's chapter, the concept 'value schizophrenia' is used to describe the contradictory situation for teachers when they find themselves caught between test results and complex individual stories. The neoliberal organisation, in which evaluations can have a direct bearing on whether teachers get to keep their jobs, makes teachers afraid to include pupils with special needs in their classes, even though these are pupils they would like to have and help as teachers. The plurality of norms becomes a frustrating situation for them that hinders their work. But the plurality of norms can also be an asset. This is evident in the example in Chapter 8, of how clandestine children in Sweden have the right to education, although their presence in the country is considered illegal. Two norms are materialised at the same time: a human rights norm asserting that every child has the right to education, and a restrictive citizenship norm which makes some people's presence in the country illegal. Reimers, in Chapter 7, claims that even in the neoliberal policy documents there exists a plurality of educational discourses and norms, which makes the neoliberal educational reforms unequivocal and less predictable than might be expected. In Chapter 3, Martinsson writes on the precarious situation for people living in a village in the Pakistani countryside, how different and often contradictory norms, even neoliberal ones, make identities and subject positions less stable. It becomes possible to imagine other sorts of societies, other possible ways to conceptualise 'I'. Instead of dismissing nationalism and neoliberalism as conditions for political subjectivity, in Chapter 5, Takayama suggests that citizenship education could make use of new definitions of nationalism in order to create conditions for democratic political subjectivity.

The above points to the unstable character of all forms of normativity. Hegemony is never total (Laclau and Mouffe 1985). Hegemony, or to use the language of Deleuze and Guattari (1988), molar lines, is always simultaneously constituted and challenged by a plethora of norms and materialities. Different assemblages are not only collections of norms. The different norms in an assemblage are entangled, contingent, affecting and making each other possible (or impossible). These entanglements mean there are many ways to inhabit and perform norms (Mahmood 2012, p. 15). It is therefore not possible to predict what subjectivity and concomitant actions will emerge from the messy processes that also involve neoliberalism. A specific interest in this book is therefore how political subjectivities are made possible in the intersections and crossroads, and the ongoing emergence of norms.

8   *Lena Martinsson and Eva Reimers*

The ways in which neoliberal norms are repeated and transformed together with other norms have implications not only for practises of education, but also for how to make sense of education and for how subject positions – as teachers, children, students, parents, activists or citizens – are made possible in educational assemblages or assemblages where education is a part (Ball 2013). This means these assemblages are messy reiterations of different norms pertaining to differing normative fields and practises and to differing sectors of society, differing ideologies and differing objectives. Thus, there is no given direction of the goal of education. This not only means that educational assemblages are contingent, it also makes it difficult, or even impossible, to ascertain one specific norm, such as the neoliberal norm, as the only decisive norm. Consequently, it becomes uncertain what subjectivities can and will emerge from different educational practises.

Outline: the chapters

The book has been planned so that the different chapters will plug into, contrast with and add new perspectives to each other. At the same time, the chapters are independent and can be read separately. The chapters show how normative materialisations are produced and performative in different places. The theme about neoliberal reiterations is discussed in a variety of places, ranging from a playground at an English school to a Pakistani village to global multilateral policy documents and Swedish school governance practises. Relations between education, the neoliberal norms and political subjectivity are also discussed from a philosophical point of view. This allows the reader to meet the ongoing emergence of neoliberalism, as well as of political subjectivity, from different vantage points. Our ambition with this disposition, and this collection of chapters, is to open up for a decentred understanding of the ongoing reiteration and production of neoliberalism

This introductory chapter is followed by an interview with Gert Biesta. A central theme in this second chapter is the distinction between a social and a political conception of citizenship. Biesta criticizes the understanding of social citizenship, common in citizenship education, for simply being a question of social cohesion. He especially rejects ideas that children should be socialised to values described as specific national values, and to ambitions of a common national identity. He also rejects the notion that acting as a democratic citizen is the same as actively contributing to the infrastructure of society. He claims that to merely support the social cohesion and the societal infrastructure is a neoliberal claim on the citizen in a time when welfare societies are being deconstructed, emphasising that a cohesive society is not necessarily a democratic society. Instead of cohesion and common identities, it is important to value plurality and find ways to live together in plurality. The point of departure for a democratic society is therefore an explicit orientation towards the democratic values of liberty, equality and solidarity. To further challenge the idea of cohesion, Biesta, with reference to Rancière, describes democracy as an event where the societal order is interrupted, questioned and confronted with the idea of equality. For these interruptions to be possible, there is a need for what Biesta describes as subjectification, which

Introduction 9

implies individual moments of dissensus, disagreement and disidentification with the society and with the social cohesion. Another theme discussed in the chapter is how to understand plurality of identities in relation to power or to what Biesta wants to denominate 'force'. The final section of the chapter focuses on the role of education in the becoming(s) of democracy.

In Chapter 3, Lena Martinsson writes on how Pakistani teachers, researchers and activists try to use education to challenge the ongoing construction of class society and subalternity. They strongly criticise the public schools' inability to teach the subaltern children and children from the lower classes to think outside the box and develop critical thinking. The teachers and activists, in line with Biesta et al. (2014) and Gayatri Chakravorty Spivak (2008), want the pupils to be able to imagine another sort of society. At the same time, neoliberal schools, with no ambition to educate pupils and students in social studies, humanities or aesthetics of importance for political subjectivity to emerge, are plugged into the Pakistani educational assemblage. It is an intervention that might merge well with the class society and with a feudal organisation in the countryside. In spite of this, Martinsson underlines the consequences of not understanding the exposed children and their communities as lacking the capacity to act as political subjects due to lack of education. The second part of the chapter discusses how a plurality of norms and normative materialities, such as neoliberalism, radical school practises and feudalism, are reiterated, affected by, merging with and transforming each other in a village and what this messiness can contribute towards the emergence of political subjectivity in the community.

In Chapter 4, Jos Harvey and Jessica Ringrose write on how neoliberalism has pervaded the English school system, from the quasi-privatisation of schools as part of an academy and free-school initiative to the audit culture enforced by panopticon inspectors in 'OFSTED' (Office for Standards in Education). Their chapter questions how equalities are situated, or rather squeezed, performed and quashed within the school system under new performative measures that have been described as benchmarks of neoliberal marketised educational reforms. To identify the ways in which equality and neoliberalism intra-act in schools, the authors draw upon research obtained through the case study of the creation of a new equalities policy at a primary school in East London. They show some of the contradictory and schizoid effects of the drive for equality objectives, which can end up invisiblising the complexity and range of equalities issues in everyday school life as well as the political subjectivity among the pupils, who describe another sort of insight, recognising an unfair and unequal situation in the school and on the playground, and make suggestions for change.

In Chapter 5, Keita Takayama uses the example of Japan to explore different ways of constructing and making use of national sentiments in education in order to make way for political subjectivity. He argues that nationalism can become a source of collective identity, which can be channelled to protect public values which are currently put under pressure by neoliberal social and economic reform. Differing from both the Japanese conservatives and the Japanese left, Takayama delineates a middle way, reclaiming nationalism as a means to arouse desire for participation in the quest for freedom, equality and solidarity in Japan.

The chapter presents an analysis of how the cold-war geopolitical context has shaped post-war politics of education in Japan. Following the war, the occupational power depoliticised education in order to prevent the ultra-nationalism of the imperial rule. Education became almost independent from state rule, and teaching about Japan was guided by the principle of neutrality. The cold-war era witnessed a struggle regarding the independence of education and the role of nationalism. In the 1990s, the Abe regime took a strong grip on education, and the notion of 'love of country' became central in the curriculum. Rather than simply rejecting this notion as excluding and problematic nationalism, Takayama proposes making use of nationalism in teaching. Through critical studies of how the nation has been, and continues to be, constructed, pupils can become aware of themselves as political subjects, taking part in the construction of the nation. The chapter concludes with a call for Asian scholars to use Asia as an anchor point in order to disrupt the cold-war spell on education politics.

Chapter 6, written by Rita Foss Lindblad and Sverker Lindblad, maps changes in governance of Swedish compulsory education and how this produces new, or different, conceptions of who the learner is and is expected to become. Drawing on Foucault, Foss Lindblad and Lindblad argue that governance produces subjectivities, and the aim of the chapter is to point to the making of the educated through different forms of education governance. They identify four phases of different forms of governance in Sweden. In the first phase, education is governed by centralised decision-making and standardised solutions of educational problems. In this period, the educated are envisioned as democratic citizens striving for social and economic well-being for themselves as well as for the state. The second phase is characterised by decentralisation. Instead of offering standardised solutions, the government decided on achievement goals that local municipalities were expected to handle. The image of the educated emerging from this is of engaged participants in local matters, that is, with a stronger focus on the individual than in the previous period. In the third phase, education governance is characterised by marketisation. A deregulated school market is created, with free school choice between different municipal as well as private schools. The idea is that school quality will improve through competition, and that the right of individuals to make rational educational choices will improve their life chances. This form of governance produces the educated as informed consumers. The fourth phase is characterised by governance by numbers. It is the global phase where international, as well as national, testing becomes the main signifier of quality in education. This governance produces the flexible and self-regulated learner. The authors make a thorough analysis of the international governance by numbers. Their conclusion is that this form of governance implies homogenisation and limitations not only on what education can be, but also on the possibilities for the emergence of political subjectivities.

The main question in Chapter 7, written by Eva Reimers, is how neoliberal educational discourses can produce differing subjectivities. Inspired by post-humanist perspectives, Reimers presents a reading of multilateral documents from the OECD, the EU and UNESCO. In reading the documents from the three organisations together, it becomes evident that they belong to the same

Introduction 11

education assemblage, an assemblage where education is intertwined with, or plugged into, the economy as well as equity and citizenship. Similar articulations of the objective of education are found in all the documents. The most evident similarity is how education plugs into the neoliberal economic market. All documents constitute education as a tool for prosperity and a better future. The value of education is dominantly constructed as monetary, both for individuals and for nation-states. The reason for nations (and individuals) to spend money and time on education is to get rich. The UNESCO documents also plug in education with human rights, which produces a slightly different flight line, opening up for other values than the economic ones, such as gender equality, social equality and sustainability. Reading the documents together evinces the presence of possible frictions and lines in all the documents that in many ways can be in conflict with the dominant economic discourse and can also disrupt the taken for granted notion of cohesiveness as the goal for every society. When education and economy are plugged into concepts such as 'democracy', 'citizenship' and 'intercultural dialogue', a more ambiguous image of the dominant neoliberal education discourse can emerge, an image that might even subvert the hegemony of the market economy in relation to education. Reimers consequently argues that even the institutionalised neoliberal educational discourse presented in multilateral organisations are messy assemblages, which offer possibilities for conceptions of education as a space where political subjectivity can emerge.

In the concluding chapter, Lena Martinsson and Eva Reimers use the preceding chapters in the book to comment and reflect on the situation in Europe 2015–2016, where at least a million of refugees are seeking security. They demonstrate that this situation raises new questions about education and political subjectivity. When people are dying in their efforts to find security in Europe or are denied human rights after managing to enter Europe, the idea of cohesive national states, or a cohesive Europe, becomes increasingly difficult to maintain. Another problem addressed in the chapter emerges from the neoliberal conception of the human subject as independent and rational, which does not take the existential and social situation of interdependence into account, making it difficult for people to emerge as compassionate and solidary fellow human beings. Salient for the present situation are simultaneous articulations and materialisations of competing and contradictory norms. From the assemblages of norms emerge at least two opposing forms of political subjectivity. One form adheres to democratic values of equality and interdependence, working towards a more open Europe and member states that respect the human rights of those who have entered, or are on their way to enter, Europe. Another political subjectivity limiting the democratic values of equality and interdependence to specific people defined as already part of the nation is the nationalist movement, struggling to close the borders and to refuse entry of refugees. With help from three empirical examples, the authors portray schools as intense spaces for political struggle between these different political subjectivities. The authors show how schools can become spaces where teachers and pupils can enact alternative understandings of a more democratic, transformative and open society.

References

Apple, M. (2002). *Globalizing education: Policies, pedagogies, & politics*. New York: P. Lang.

Ball, S.J. (2006). *Education policy and social class*. London: Routledge.

Ball, S.J. (2012). *Global education inc*. London: Routledge.

Ball, S.J. (2013). *Foucault, power, and education*. London: Routledge.

Biesta. G. (2014). *The beautiful risk of education*. Boulder, CO: Paradigm Publishers.

Biesta, G.J.J., Allan, J. and Edwards, R.G. (Eds.) (2014). *Making a difference in theory: The theory question in education and the education question in theory*. London & New York: Routledge.

Brown, W. (2015). *Undoing the demos: Neoliberalism's stealth revolution*. New York: Zone Books.

Buras, K.L. and Apple, M.W. (2005). School choice, neoliberal promises, and unpromising evidence. *Educational Policy* 19(3): 550–564.

Butler, J. (2004). *Undoing gender*. London: Routledge.

Butler, J. (2015). *Notes toward a performative theory of assembling*. London: Harvard University Press.

Connell, R. (2013). The neoliberal cascade and education: An essay on the market agenda and its consequences. *Critical Studies in Education* 54(2): 99–112.

Davies, B. and Bansel, P. (2007). Neoliberalism and education. *International Journal of Qualitative Studies in Education* 20(3): 247–259.

Deleuze, G. and Guattari, F. (1988). *A thousand plateaus: Capitalism and schizophrenia* [Mille plateaux]. London: Athlone.

Grewal, I. (2005). *Transnational America: Feminisms, diasporas, neoliberalisms*. Durham: Duke University Press.

Harvey, D. (2006). *Spaces of global capitalism*, London: Verso.

Laclau, E. and Mouffe, C. (1985). *Hegemony and socialist strategy*. London and New York: Verso.

Lindblad, S. and Popkewitz, T. (Eds.) (2004). *Educational restructuring, international perspectives on traveling policies*. Greenwich: Information Age Publishing.

Mahmood, S. (2012). *Politics of piety: The Islamic revival and the feminist subject*. Princeton, NJ: Princeton University Press.

Martinsson, L. and Reimers, E. (2007). Towards a disharmonious pluralism: Discourse analysis of official discourses about social diversity. In A. Lin (Ed.). *Problematizing identity: Everyday struggles in language, culture and education* (pp. 51–65). London and New York: Lawrence Erlbaum.

Martinsson, L. and Reimers, E. (2010). *Norm-struggles: Sexualities in contentions*. Newcastle upon Tyne: Cambridge Scholars Publishing.

Massey, D. (2005). *For space*. Los Angeles: Sage Publications.

Meyer, H. and Benavot, A. (2013). *PISA, power, and policy: The emergence of global educational governance*. Didcot: Symposium Books.

Mouffe, C. (2005). *On the political*. New York: Routledge.

OECD (2016). *About the OECD*. http://www.oecd.org/about. Retrieved 6 March 2016.

Rofel, L. (2007). *Desiring China: Experiments in neoliberalism, sexuality, and public Culture*. Durham: Duke University Press.

Spivak, G.C. (2008). *Other Asias*. Oxford: Blackwell Publishing.

Swedish National Agency of Education (2009). *Vad påverkar resultaten i svensk grundskola?* [What influences achievements in Swedish compulsory education?]. Stockholm: Fritzes.

Swedish National Agency of Education (2012). *Likvärdig utbildning i svensk grund-skola?* [Equal education in Swedish compulsory education?]. Stockholm: Fritzes.

UNESCO (2016). *About us.* http://en.unesco.org/about-us/introducing-unesco. Retrieved 6 March 2016.

Youdell, D. (2006). Diversity, inequality, and a post-structural politics for education. *Discourse: Studies in the Cultural Politics of Education* 27(1): 33–42.

Youdell, D. (2011). *School trouble.* Abingdon and New York: Routledge.

2 Politics, subjectivity and education in neoliberal times

An interview with Gert Biesta

Gert Biesta, Lena Martinsson and Eva Reimers

There are several reasons why we wanted to do an interview with Gert Biesta. We are ourselves very much inspired by his way of theorising the differences between socialisation and subjectification. It has become an important input into our way of thinking about political subjectivity. However, on reading his texts in relation to feminist and intersectional perspectives, several questions emerged. We thus wanted to know more about how Biesta thought on subjectivity in connection to power, identity, agency and his conception of plurality in relation to democracy.

The present chapter evolves around four main topics. We begin by asking questions about different conceptions of citizenship and how this relates to democracy and political subjectivity. The following part is centred around the concept of dissensus, which is crucial in Biesta's understanding of the possibility for political or democratic subjectivity. In the next part, Biesta develops this further by expanding on how the notion of subjectivity relates to individuality, identity, collectives and institutions. The final section of the chapter focuses on the role of education in the becoming(s) of democracy.

Social and political conceptions of citizenship

Q. In several of your publications on education, democracy and citizenship, including your book *Learning Democracy in School and Society* (2011), you have emphasised the importance of the distinction between a social and a political conception of citizenship. Can you say a bit more about this distinction and why you consider it to be important?

GB. The reason why I find it important to make this distinction has a lot to do with the way in which over the past 15 years or so citizenship has been defined and approached in policy documents, including education policy, and in research that is supposed to underpin such policies. What I have found interesting, and in a sense even remarkable, is that the question of citizenship is often posed as the question of *social cohesion*. Based on the claim that contemporary society is apparently insufficiently cohesive, politicians highlight the need for educational interventions that connect children and young people more closely to society – turning them into 'good citizens', as it is sometimes called. There are more 'extreme' versions of this trend where it is argued, for

Politics, subjectivity and education 15

example, that children and young people should subscribe to certain national values. In Britain there was, for example, a call for everyone to subscribe to British values – which of course immediately leads to the question of what such values are and how British they actually are. But the link between citizenship and social cohesion can also be found in the idea of 'active citizenship', which often means no more than that children, young people and again all citizens, should make an active contribution to the infrastructure of society.

Q. What do you see as the problem there?

GB. It may, of course, be a good idea to make the point John F. Kennedy made long ago – 'Ask not what your country can do for you, but ask what you can do for your country' – but there are two things that are important here. One thing not to forget is that the whole discourse of active citizenship emerged at a time when the welfare state was in rapid decline – some would say when it was rapidly being dismantled, partly because of a lack of money but partly also for ideological reasons such as the conservative belief in the small state or Margaret Thatcher's claim that such a thing as society does not even exist. In this sense the call for active citizenship is a typical neoliberal move where individuals are being made responsible for what used to be seen as a responsibility of the state. The other thing not to forget, and that brings me to my distinction, is that a cohesive society is not necessarily or automatically also a democratic society – and we can easily think of societies that are extremely cohesive, where all the noses point in the same direction, but where, precisely for this reason, democracy is entirely absent; North Korea is one example that comes to mind. The issue here is that a democratic society is not just a society that in some way hangs together or where citizens are active, but is a society that is explicitly orientated towards the democratic values of liberty, equality and solidarity.

One way to understand the difference between the social and the political understanding of citizenship, then, is in terms of how each looks at plurality and difference. The social understanding of citizenship tends to see plurality and difference predominantly as a *problem*, as something that troubles and threatens the stability of society, and therefore as something that needs to be addressed and, to a certain extent, even needs to be overcome. That is why on this end of the spectrum we encounter a discourse of society falling apart, and a focus on citizenship as having to do with common values, national identity, pro-social behaviour, care for one's neighbour and so on. In the political understanding of citizenship, on the other hand, plurality and difference are seen as the very *raison d'être* of democratic processes and practises and therefore as what needs to be protected and cultivated with reference to the values of liberty, equality and solidarity.

Q. Some people might say that this implies that a democratic society is also based on certain values, and although these are different from nationalistic values such as the British values you mention, there is nonetheless a set of values that democratic citizens should 'sign up' for. So how different are the social and the political conceptions of citizenship actually?

16 *Gert Biesta et al.*

GB. Again, there are two points that are important here. One is that democracy is not just about any set of values, but is about a set of values that provides a 'framing' for the question of how we can live together in plurality on the assumption that plurality is in principle desirable. This, for me, is one of the key intuitions of the democratic way of sorting out our collective lives, namely from the idea that plurality is not a problem that needs to be 'solved' but is something we should value. There are weaker and stronger justifications for this but they all come back to two of the three democratic values – on the one hand the value of freedom, that is, that every human being should have the freedom to live their life in the way they deem valuable or meaningful, and on the other hand the value of equality, that is, that everyone should have this right. In this regard I do think that the values of democracy, although they are values, are of a fundamentally different 'order' than nationalistic values such as Britishness, which actually try to reduce plurality.

The second point – which is more philosophical – has to do with the question of whether it is actually possible or meaningful to think of democracy as an identifiable and definable order.

Q. Can you say a bit more about this?

GB. One way to see what the point here is, is by acknowledging, as I argue in my work, that there is nothing natural about democracy – which also means that there is nothing rational about democracy. Democracy is a particular historical invention, and although over the centuries many people may have come to see it as a desirable way to deal with the question of governing under the condition of plurality, there are no compelling reasons for democracy, at least not until one is committed to the underlying values of liberty, equality and solidarity. The idea of government 'of the people, by the people, and for the people' – Abraham Lincoln's famous definition – is, after all, only an interesting option if one cares about the people, and if one cares about *all* people and their freedom in an equal manner. In this respect I agree with Chantal Mouffe who, against certain tendencies in liberal political philosophy to 'naturalise' democracy, has argued that democracy is a thoroughly *political* project (2005). This means that a choice for democracy is neither rational nor irrational – it simply is a choice. While we may well be able to give reasons for the desirability of democracy – and here we might favour Winston Churchill's 'minimal' definition of democracy as the worst form of government except for all other forms tried so far – the reasons we give only carry weight for those who are committed to its underlying values. This is why those who oppose democracy – and again this is a point I got from Mouffe, and I find it really helpful and important – should not be seen as irrational but simply as opposing democracy. In more theoretical terms we can say that we should be mindful that the division between rationality and irrationality does not automatically or necessarily coincide with the division between democracy and its 'outside'.

Q. What does that imply for the question of whether democracy is an 'order', as you put it?

Politics, subjectivity and education 17

GB. To say that democracy is a thoroughly political project implies that it cannot be inclusive of everything and everyone. Mouffe makes this point by saying that democracy is not a 'pluralism without any frontiers', in that a democratic society cannot treat those who put its basic institutions and values into question as legitimate adversaries (Mouffe 2000). This does not mean, however, that the borders of the democratic community can only be drawn in one way and that the democratic order within these borders is fixed. This is what Mouffe expresses with her idea of democracy as a 'conflictual consensus'. She describes this as the situation where there is consensus about what she characterises as the 'ethico-political values of liberty and equality' – and note that unlike me, Mouffe doesn't put solidarity in the mix – but where there is dissent about their interpretation, that is, about what these values mean in concrete situations.

For Mouffe, the line to be drawn, therefore, is between those who reject those values outright and those who, while accepting them, fight for different and sometimes conflicting interpretations and articulations. So any particular democratic 'settlement' can only ever be one particular democratic 'hegemony', to use Mouffe's term, that is, one particular way in which the values of liberty and equality, and the inevitable tension between the two, is negotiated and acted out (Mouffe 2000). So whereas Mouffe does acknowledge that those who oppose the values of liberty and equality are clearly outside of the political project of democracy – which doesn't make them irrational, but does highlight that they have different political values – this doesn't mean that those who do subscribe to these values can only come to one resolution about how these values should be made concrete, which for Mouffe, if I understand her correctly, particularly has to do with the inevitable tension between liberty and equality. Mouffe's work thus acts as a reminder that there may always be the possibility of a different democracy, and perhaps also of a better democracy – and when we look at the history of democracy we can see clear shifts and transitions. Think, for example, of what, over time, has happened with the right to vote and stand for election.

Democracy as the staging of dissensus

Q. Besides Mouffe, you also engage with these issues through the work of Jacques Rancière. Can you say more about where you see his contribution to the discussion?

GB. There are two insights from Rancière that I find helpful for the discussion – and both are, in a sense, counterintuitive but do make quite a lot of sense in my view. The first has to do with his suggestion that no social order – or, with the particular term Rancière uses: no 'police order' – can ever be fully equal (Rancière 2003). While in some societies or social configurations there may be more equality – or less inequality – than in others, the very way in which the social is structured precludes the possibility of full equality, or at least makes it highly unlikely. In contrast to Mouffe, however, Rancière maintains that every social order is *all-inclusive* in that in any given order everyone has a particular

18 *Gert Biesta et al.*

place, role and identity. But this does not mean – and this is crucial – that everyone is included in the ruling of the order. After all, women, children, slaves and immigrants had a clear place and identity in the democracy of Athens, namely as those who were not allowed to participate in the decision-making about the polis. Rancière uses the interesting phrase that they were 'included as excluded'. Against this background Rancière then defines 'politics' – which for him is always *democratic* politics – as the interruption of an existing social order with reference to the idea of equality. Politics, as the interruption of a particular order in which everyone has a place, is therefore manifest in actions that, as he puts it, reconfigure the space where parties have been defined. Politics, as an interruption of an existing order, therefore makes visible what had no business being seen and makes heard a discourse where, as he puts it, before there was only 'noise'.

One implication of this way of looking at democracy is that we can no longer think of democracy as a particular regime, way of life or state of society. Rather, democracy becomes an event, that is, the moment where the particular way in which society is ordered is confronted with the idea of equality, when a particular social order is interrupted with reference to the idea of equality. Rancière refers to this encounter as 'dissensus', as it is about two logics that do not fit with each other – or in more philosophical terms, that are incommensurable. There is on the one hand the social logic of inequality and on the other hand the political logic of equality. It is the moment where the demand for equality meets a particular and always unequal social situation that democracy occurs, but not as a state of affairs but as the interruption of a state of affairs (Rancière 2003). That's why we might refer to Rancière's conception of democracy as a sporadic conception of democracy – democracy is not 'there' all the time. That's why it's actually more appropriate to think of it as a theory of *democratisation*. Democratisation, as an event, does not turn an unequal society into an equal society – because total equality is, according to Rancière and I think he is right, a sheer impossibility. But the change in the social order that may be the result of this may nonetheless result in a social order that is seen as more equal, or, with a phrase that may sound a bit odd but is actually more accurate, a social order that is seen as 'better equal'.

Q. Can you give an example of this process?

GB. One of the examples Rancière gives is about voting rights and particularly the situation where women claim the right to vote in a system that excludes them from voting. The point here is, and this is the second really interesting aspect of Rancière's work, that this claim should not be understood as a request for inclusion into the existing order. The reason for this is because women who are claiming the right to vote in a system that excludes them from voting – a system in which the idea that you are female and that you have the right to vote simply makes no sense; it can only be perceived as 'noise', we could say – are not after an identity that already exists. They are thus making a claim for the very identity that is impossible in the existing social order. The claim is precisely in this sense a moment of dissensus because it introduces, in the existing order, something that is heterogeneous to it, as Rancière puts it. If this claim is successful – and there is of course an important question of who decides – the outcome is not that more people are now included in the existing order. What rather takes place is a reordering in which a previously impossible identity – female and having the right to vote – now becomes a possible identity. This is why Rancière argues – and I find this insight really helpful for the whole question of civic education – that democratisation is not a process of identification, that is, of taking up an existing identity, but is rather a process of disidentification or, with the term that I think is key here, a process of *subjectification* – a process of being a subject of politics or a political subject. So here we have something that we might call the 'birth' of democratic agency, and the key insight from Rancière is that such agency is always 'out of order' – it is always in tension with the existing order, putting a challenge to what is possible in that order.

An individual conception of political subjectivity?

Q. Does the emphasis on subjectification imply that political subjectivities are always individual or is it possible to understand political subjectivity as a collective act as well?

GB. As a 'technical' point I would say that political subjectivity is always individual – and I mean 'technical' here in the sense that I would claim that only an individual can be a subject; I can't see how a collective can be a subject. But that doesn't mean that political action is only individual or, more specifically, that we should think of it exclusively in terms of one individual standing up against the system. On the contrary, much political action in the way in which Rancière describes it – that is, as a staging of dissensus – is done by groups rather than by individuals. So although the key point that I would like to make with Rancière is about the importance of the difference between thinking of democratic politics as identification or as subjectification – and the preference is for the latter view – that doesn't mean that political action is by definition individual.

Let me take the opportunity to make another point here as well, because in the examples Rancière gives there is a bit of a tendency to focus on a rather heroic act by an individual or group of individuals that in some way then results in a reordering of the police order, that is, of a particular distribution of identities (Rancière uses the more abstract phrase 'distribution of the sensible', that is, a distribution of what can be seen, perceived and articulated). There are indeed examples of such events, but in addition to the qualitative 'turn' that such events seem to effectuate, we shouldn't underestimate the importance of quantity and repetition. To put it differently, it is one thing for one person to stage dissensus, but when others follow, or when dissensus is staged by a larger group, it tends to have more force – that's the point of quantity. The point of repetition is to highlight that quite often the staging of dissensus is not something that will immediately 'flip' a system, but when such stagings are being repeated over time they also gain force.

20 *Gert Biesta et al.*

Q. We wonder how you theorise the relations between power and politics. We can't see much of power relations in the way you write about politics. This is a big difference compared to Mouffe. How do you conceptualise power?

GB. I would say that the previous comments about dissensus, quantity and repetition give some insights into the role of power – though you will have noticed that I use the word 'force' rather than 'power', mainly because 'force' is a slightly more descriptive word, whereas 'power' has of course become a concept with a complicated theoretical history! But even if that's granted I am never really sure whether any account of power – be it theoretical or be it empirical – adds much to our understanding. Sometimes it takes very little power – or perhaps force is the better word here – to create significant changes. In other cases, all the power of the world turns out to be unable to make much of a (democratic) difference. So where power comes from, what turns out to have power is difficult to predict – which means that many analyses of power only make sense 'after the event' but not necessarily before. By this I'm not saying that politics is an entirely rational process – on the contrary, what counts as rational is crucially dependent on a particular socio-political 'hegemony' – but that doesn't mean that politics is just a process of force against force where the strongest is the winner. This may be the dynamics of the social, but for me this is not the dynamics of the political if – in line with Mouffe and Rancière – we understand the political in relation to democracy and democratisation, that is, connected to very specific issues (living together in plurality) and values (equality, liberty and solidarity).

Q. In your work, political subjectivity seems mostly to be present outside of political institutions. What are your thoughts about political subjectivity within political institutions?

GB. There is indeed an anarchic streak to my thinking – where I take anarchic literally as the absence of an 'arche' or structure – but that doesn't mean that institutions do not matter. My thinking here is similar to what I have said before about power, I think. One important point – and here I take inspiration from Arendt, but also Derrida – is that institutions in themselves are nothing (Derrida 1992). They can only work if, in some way, we invest in them, that is, if in our actions we give them the power they need in order to work. Corruption is a good example of where this goes wrong, because if in our everyday interactions we do not respect the institutions that are supposed to support and protect us, we are immediately eroding such institutions. This means that for me institutions are very important, but they cannot do the work for us – they can only work if we constantly invest in them. This is where I see an important connection between the micro and the macro.

Now with regard to the more 'technical' question of whether political subjectivity can exist within political institutions, I would like to respond in terms of the distinction between identity and subjectivity and would like to say that within political institutions there are clearly defined and identifiable identities, and such identities make certain ways of acting and being possible. Along with Rancière I would like to retain the word 'subjectivity' for those political moments that are outside of the existing field of identities, that interrupt the particular order of identities. So that doesn't mean that there is nothing to do within political institutions and that all political acting and being takes place outside of such institutions, but it does highlight that there is also something about the dynamics of politics that cannot be understood within the confines of institutions.

Q. You seem to use the concepts of political subjectivity, democratic agency and citizenship as almost synonymous. What are the important aspects of these concepts, and how do they relate to each other?

As you may have noticed, my preference lies with the notion of political subjectivity, where 'political' for me refers to democratic politics. So 'democratic subjectivity' would be another option here. The reason why I find this an important notion is because I think one of the key questions for me is what it means to be a democratic subject, which I see as a rather different question from that of what it means to have a democratic identity – and the key lies in the word 'have', where I think that identities are indeed 'things' we have, whereas subjectivity is about how we are, exist and act. The notion of agency refers to the active dimension of political subjectivity, which is a reason I sometimes use it. But the problem with agency is that it has a very specific meaning within sociological discussions, which is the main reason I try to stay away from it – mainly because my approach is not a sociological one. Citizenship has, of course, a clear technical meaning, in that you can only be a citizen of something – and the 'something' is in most cases a nation state. So citizenship in this regard refers to a particular relationship between individuals and nation states. There is a question of whether such nation states have to be thought of as democratic – I'm inclined to veer towards that position as I find it a little difficult to think of being a citizen of a state where you have no rights, for example. There are also less technical ways in which the notions of citizen and citizenship are being used, and then they come closer to political actors (or perhaps political subjects). The discourse of global citizenship seems to disconnect the idea of the citizen from that of the nation state and points to a more encompassing political identity. I think that the main question for me is how within existing discourses on citizenship – and more importantly from my own perspective, citizenship education – we can make sure that citizenship is understood in political rather than social terms, which brings us back to where we started!

Q. Before we turn to the question of education, there is one more question we would like to ask about political subjectivity, which has to do with the work of Butler. Butler writes about the importance of recognition and recognising oneself in the world – a view that, we think, has many similarities with Arendt and her suggestion that one becomes someone in plurality and that one can be met in this uniqueness. For Butler, it is an important point that not everyone will be seen, or be met, that not everyone will be recognised, and this moment of un-recognition is a moment of conflict and friction. Is it impossible for this

22 *Gert Biesta et al.*

person to be a political subject? Could not the experience of not being recognised, not recognising oneself, lead to political activism? Is the meeting with the other necessary? And if so, who is the other? Who is the person, or persons or groups that meet the other? Is it the teacher, the schoolmate, someone who can recognise the situation of not being recognised, like one who identifies herself with the one who is supposed to be met?

GB. I agree that the experience of what we might call not being recognised – but I will come back to that in a minute – can be an important motivator for political action. One could say that such an experience makes visible that in the particular 'distribution of the sensible' particular identities have no place. Now before I say more about the political dynamics that may emerge from this, I do wish to highlight that some identities have no place in a particular democratic hegemony because they are against the values that constitute democratic politics. So democracy does not mean that *any* identity should get a place on the 'inside', so to speak. In this regard I wish to emphasise the importance of seeing democracy as a thoroughly political project – and hence with its own political normativity – and not as an administrative system that is just after giving everyone any voice. If you then ask, as you did in your question, whether it is important for such a person to be a political subject, I would say 'on the contrary,' but the difference that is relevant here is again that between identity and subjectivity, as we could say that Butler describes a situation where particular identities are not possible – or, from the perspective of individuals, the given identities do not 'fit' (think of the example of women and voting rights).

What I like about Rancière's ideas – or the way I try to understand them – is that he shows that the real problem is not that some people are excluded from existing identities, because in that case it would just be a matter for the majority to 'welcome' those people into those identities, if that phrase makes sense. The problem is, in other words, not a question of inclusion, but requires a transformation of what Rancière calls the police order, so that *different* identities become possible. Engaging in the struggle for such a transformation is the moment of political subjectification. The other point to make here is about the notion of recognition – although this is probably less directed at Butler than at the philosophy of recognition that can, for example, be found in the work of Axel Honneth (Honneth 1992). If we think of the democratic problem as one where majorities 'recognise' minorities, there's not only the problem that such recognition can only take place within a field that is already known, so to speak, that is, a field where the identities are already defined. Also, the politics of recognition remains caught in a master-slave dialectic, where the act of recognition remains an act of power (sometimes presented as generosity or benevolence) on the part of the ones who are in power towards the ones who are not in power. In this sense the call for recognition doesn't address the underlying distribution of power, and actually gives power to those in the centre.

Education and the experiment of democracy

Q. You emphasise in your work that your interest is not in political theory or political philosophy, but in education. Nonetheless, you spend quite a lot of

Politics, subjectivity and education 23

time on theoretical and philosophical themes rather than starting directly with the educational questions. Why is that so?

GB. You are right that my interest is indeed in the educational dimensions of all this, and for that reason I could, of course, start where almost everyone who talks about the relationship between citizenship, learning and education seems to start, that is, by suggesting that civic learning and democratic education have to do with the acquisition of the knowledge, skills and dispositions that are needed for good citizenship. Yet the reason why I do not start and cannot start from there is twofold.

It first of all has to do with the fact that the meaning of citizenship is contested – and perhaps it could even be argued that the meaning of citizenship is *essentially* contested, which means that the contestation over what good citizenship is is actually part and parcel of what democracy is about. I have shown that there is not only discussion about whether citizenship should be understood as a social or as a political identity, but have also made it clear that amongst those who see citizenship as fundamentally a political identity – which is the position I take as well – there are still different views about what good citizenship is. More importantly, so I wish to suggest, there are also different views about whether citizenship is a positive identity – that is, an identity that can be positively identified and articulated – or whether citizenship is to be understood as a process of disidentification, as a moment of political agency that is always necessarily 'out of order'.

The second reason why I do not and cannot start with enlisting the knowledge, skills and dispositions that need to be learned in order to become a good citizen has to do with the fact that, unlike what many seem to assume, the way in which we understand the learning involved in citizenship is not neutral with regard to how we understand citizenship itself. It is not, therefore, that we can simply go to learning theory for the learning and to political theory for the citizenship and then weld the two together to create civic learning. The point here is that as long as we see citizenship as a positive, identifiable identity, we can indeed see the learning involved as a process of the acquisition of the knowledge, skills and dispositions that are needed to bring out this identity – or, to put it from the other side, the knowledge, skills and dispositions that are needed to bring newcomers into the existing socio-political order. If, on the other hand, the moment of democracy is a moment of disidentification with the existing socio-political order, and if it is the case that it is in this moment that the democratic subject emerges, then the position and nature of the learning involved change. This is why I have suggested making a distinction between a *socialisation* conception of civic learning – which is about the learning necessary to become part of an existing socio-political order – and a *subjectification* conception of civic learning – which is about the learning that is involved in engagement with what we might refer to as the 'experiment' of democracy. Whereas a socialisation conception of civic learning is about learning *for future citizenship*, the subjectification conception of civic learning is about learning *from current citizenship*, from current experiences with and engagement in the ongoing experiment of democracy.

24 *Gert Biesta et al.*

Q. What is the reason for referring to democracy as an 'experiment'?

GB. I use the phrase the 'experiment of democracy' in order to highlight the necessarily open character of democracy. While I agree with Mouffe that democracy cannot and should not be entirely 'an-archic' – that is, without any form – I do believe, with Mouffe and with Rancière, that the democratic process needs to remain fundamentally open towards the possibility not only of *more* democracy but also of *different* democracy, of a different distribution of parts and places, of a reconfiguration of democratic identities and subjectivities, bearing in mind, as I have said earlier, that we are talking about *democratic* identities and subjectivities, and hence identities and subjectivities that are linked to democracy as a normative project. To think of democracy as an ongoing and never-ending experiment is a way to capture this idea.

While there is a lot to say about the dynamics of democratic experimentation, one thing that I wish to emphasise is the idea that the democratic experiment should be understood as a process of *transformation*. And perhaps the most important transformation that is at stake in the experiment of democracy is the transformation of 'private troubles' into 'public issues' – to use the phrase of C. Wright Mills (Mills 1959). By characterising democracy as a process of transformation, I distinguish myself from conceptions that see democracy purely in aggregative terms, that is, as a mathematical number game in which only the largest number counts and where minorities just need to adjust themselves to the majority. For me democracy entails as much a concern for the majority as it entails a concern for minorities which, after all, are only minorities because of the construction of a particular majority.

But the bigger point here is that the democratic experiment needs to be understood as having an orientation towards collective interests and the common good – or common goods. It needs to be understood as having an orientation towards the issues of the public – the *res publica*. What is always at stake, therefore, in the democratic experiment is the question of to what extent and in what form private 'wants' – that which is desired by individuals or groups – can be supported as collective needs – that is, can be considered desirable at the level of the collective, given the plurality of individual wants and always limited resources. This is not only a process where, as Zygmunt Bauman has put it, 'private problems are translated into the language of public issues' but also where 'public solutions are sought, negotiated and agreed for private troubles' (Bauman 2000). To think about the democratic experiment in terms of transformation not only means that people's *issues* become transformed. As I have tried to highlight with Rancière, the engagement with the democratic experiment also transforms *people*, most importantly in that it has the potential to engender democratic subjectivity and political agency.

Q. Is there any learning involved in such experiments?

GB. I think so. But the learning that is at stake is not about the acquisition of the knowledge, skills and dispositions needed to engage with the experiment in a 'proper' manner, most importantly because, being an experiment, it is never entirely clear what a proper way to engage with this experiment would look like. That is why we should conceive of civic learning in the subjectifica-tion mode as a process that is *non-linear*: it does not lead in a linear way from a state of *not* being a citizen to being a citizen, but fluctuates with people's actual experiences of citizenship and with their engagement in democratic experiments. We should also think of this learning as *recursive*: what is being learned is not just stored somewhere but is always fed back into action. And while it is non-linear, civic learning in the subjectification mode is definitely *cumulative*: experiences from the past cannot simply be eradicated or over-written, but continue to play a role in future experiences and actions. The latter point is particularly important because engagement with the experiment of democracy will generate both positive and negative experiences. We should not expect, therefore, that engagement with the democratic experiment will always strengthen the desire for democratic ways of acting and being – the opposite can be the case as well.

Q. Could you be more specific on what it would mean, for example, for school-ing, to enact the experiment of democracy? What about subject positions such as teacher, student, race, gender, high-performing students, low-performing students, students with special needs etcetera?

GB. The experiment of democracy is always concerned with the question of how to make living together in plurality possible with reference to the values of equality, liberty and solidarity. To live together with reference to such values – and reference sounds rather formal; perhaps we could also talk about a com-mitment to those values – raises an important and, from the perspective of the individual, often difficult question, which is the question of to what extent and in what way all our individual wants and desires can be 'sustained' collectively. The democratic question in this sense always emerges as an interruptive ques-tion – a question that interrupts our wants and desires and asks from each of us an examination of our wants and desires and most likely a certain limiting of our wants and desires. On the one hand I can think of quite a lot of moments in the daily life of schools where this question arises. After all, not everything is possible for everyone at any moment in time – so in classrooms, smaller groups, the school as a whole there is always the question of the relationship between individual wants and desires and what can be and ought to be 'car-ried' by the collective. I think what is important from the perspective of the educators in such situations is that they 'stage' the problem as a democratic problem – if, of course, they are interested in seeing the school as a place where the experiment of democracy can be conducted, or, in a formulation that I think is slightly better, as a place where it's possible to practise (with) the experiment of democracy.

One point I would like to add is that such practicing should not be confined to that of, say, collective decision-making. That's where I actually often have concerns when schools try to engage with democracy, that is, that they think that they need to construct mini-parliaments or something like that, and also that they think that democracy is a matter of debating, of coming up with rational arguments and the like. All this may have a place, but it's not the only

26   *Gert Biesta et al.*

way in which schools can serve the democratic cause, and sometimes such forms can get in the way of what needs to be taken care of as well. One thing that is often not on the radar where it concerns schools and democracy is precisely with regard to the question of how we become better at interrogating, limiting and transforming our own wants and desires, so that they can sustain a 'living together in plurality'. I see a rather strong tendency in contemporary education to go in the opposite direction and organise education – flexibly and in a personalised way – around the wants and desires of children and young people. Perhaps the most extreme manifestation of this is the idea of the student as customer and, as a result of this, the idea that educational institutions should always meet the needs of the customers, that is, give them what they want. That for me is the opposite of the logic of education, which always needs to bring in the question of whether what anyone says that he or she wants is actually what they should want – and this is in a fundamental way not only the educational question, but also the democratic question.

The phrase 'living together in plurality' may sound easy, but it is perhaps the most difficult thing to do – yet it is at the heart of what I think democracy as a political project means and aims for. The reason for connecting this to questions of wants and desires is to move the discussion away from questions of power and subjection and turn the question back to ourselves – where democracy comes with a demand, so we might say, to interrogate our desires and limit ourselves. This is a risky business, and cynics might say that if you put yourself in a vulnerable position, those with more power will simply take over. There is little to say in response to that, other than to point at examples where it was actually weakness, not force, that turned out to be the most powerful – if for a moment we can play with the distinction between force and power here. Nelson Mandela comes to mind; Gandhi perhaps; and of course, the many people who do small things that are hidden from view.

Q. You place quite a strong emphasis on people's wants and desires. Can you say a bit more about what you have in mind there? And how should we understand this in relation to the phrase you just used, that of strengthening the desire for democratic ways of acting and being?

GB. Perhaps just to clarify: when I talk about wants and desires, I do not only mean material wants and desires, although it may sound like this, but would also include immaterial wants and desires. For me this would also include the desire for a particular identity, and I think that contemporary identity politics can – partly, not totally – also be read in relation to this, that is, as the idea that every individual has a right to its 'own' identity. The 'own' here needs to be in quotation marks, in order to show that if we talk about identity in this way, it can quickly become a commodity, a thing we have or possess, rather than something we are. But my main point here is that in the democratic way of living together we should also be willing to interrogate our desire for a particular identity, which may mean that we need to limit our identity a little in order to sustain our living together. It's perhaps a rather long way of saying that for me democracy raises a more difficult question than that of recognising identities.

Politics, subjectivity and education   27

In this regard, Rancière's claim that subjectification is disidentification also turns back to ourselves – to be a political subject means that it's unlikely for our identities to remain 'untouched'. With this I am not suggesting that identity doesn't matter – and it does matter particularly in those contexts and histories where particular identities have had no opportunity to exist at all. But the democratic challenge doesn't stop there.

Q. And the desire for democracy?

GB. The reason I use that phrase stems from my observation that democracy is neither natural nor rational. It is of course rational for those who 'believe' in democracy, but for those who do not start from such a belief, it is, I think, very difficult, if not impossible to be convinced through rational argumentation that they should be(come) democratic. And in what I have said about the way in which democracy always asks us to interrogate our desires, you can also see that at an individual level it may go against what appears to us as natural. That's why the educational task – which ultimately for me is also a political task, or the educative task of politics – is to arouse a desire for this way of living together, perhaps by trying to show that in the longer term it is the more sustainable way of living together or by pointing at historical situations where things have gone dramatically wrong.

Q. This brings us to the last theme in your work, which is the idea of the public sphere and of public places more generally. We are curious to hear more about your conception of the public sphere and also whether the school can be such a public place.

GB. The idea of the public sphere is perhaps a slightly more helpful notion than that of public place, although both in a sense seem to refer to particular locations. That would be my first point: that while the notion of public place often conjures images of town squares, marketplaces, parks, of the Greek agora or the Roman forum, the question of whether such spaces can be characterised as *public* places does not so much have to do with what they look like as with what is *possible* in such locations. Here I want to suggest that what makes a place public is precisely the extent to which it makes the transformation of private wants into collective needs possible, that is, whether it is a place or location where private wants and desires can be interrogated and collectively transformed. Places are public to the extent that the experiment of democracy can take place – and while some locations may be more conducive for this than others, it's not the location in itself that is the issue here.

David Marquand's book *Decline of the Public* is helpful here, because he highlights that the public domain, as he calls it, should be understood as a *dimension* of social life, not a sector of it (Marquand 2004). He calls it a 'set of activities' with its own norms and decision rules. Marquand emphasises that the public domain is not only *different* from the private domain 'of love, friendship and personal connection' and from the market domain of 'buying and selling [and] interest and incentive', but is also *separate* from these domains. This is why he defines the public domain as 'a space, protected from

28 *Gert Biesta et al.*

the adjacent market and private domains, where strangers encounter each other as equal partners in the common life of the society'. And the key function of the public domain is to define the public interest and to produce public goods, which implies – in line with what I have said so far – that the values 'that sustain, and are sustained by, the public domain' are not the values of self-interest but of collective interest. Given that collective interest may sometimes go against one's immediate self-interest, engagement with and commitment to the public domain implies and requires 'a certain discipline' and 'a certain self-restraint'. Interestingly, Marquand argues this does not come naturally but has to be 'learned and then internalised, sometimes painfully', again in line with what I have just said.

Q. By defining public places in this way, as free from the market, as not private, you seem to depict it as a rather utopian place. Is there a danger that such places are a fiction? And why do things have to be so neat? Why don't you think that the market and the private domain can be possible places for democratic experiments?

GB. One thing to highlight is that public places are not locations, but the phrase rather refers to a certain quality of human relationships. In this regard, the quality that makes such relationships public – or we can also say political or democratic – is that they are orientated towards the interrogation of desires in light of the democratic values of equality, liberty and solidarity and with the ambition to make living in plurality possible. That's a very different quality from the relationships that characterise the domain of the market, which is precisely not about interrogating desires but rather fulfilling desires, and in contemporary capitalist economies I would also say that markets are about increasing and multiplying desires. (If we want more, we need to buy more, so the economy can keep growing.) I think that something similar can be said about the private sphere, which we could characterise as the sphere where we can 'have' our identities and are not under the demand to interrogate and transform them – though there is a question of where and how such a sphere exists, which means again that the private sphere should not be understood as a location but as a way of being – and in the case of the private, it's a way of being on one's own or with oneself. This does not mean that 'the home' is private in this sense or that 'the street' is public. It all depends on what's taking place. But I do wish to acknowledge that it is not possible to constantly question and interrupt our desires – and the point is also, as mentioned, that it's not to get rid of our desires but to transform our desires so that they can sustain living together in plurality.

Q. How does neoliberalism fit into this analysis?

GB. I would say that neoliberalism is precisely the situation where the distinctions between the different modes of being and being together are denied – which we see particularly with regard to the idea that the logic of the market should rule in all domains of our lives. When we turn citizens into consumers of public services, government into providers of public services and then create a whole set of quangos to 'quality control' what's happening in this market, we have redefined the relationship between citizens and the state from a political relationship into an economic relationship and in doing so have both redefined (and depoliticised) what it means to be a citizen and what the state means. That is why 'choice' is such a dangerous word in the context of democracy, because choice for me is basically a concept within the economic logic of the market – where we express our choices and try to get what we want – whereas in the democratic logic of the public sphere, there is always the need to interrogate our choices in light of the ambition to live together in plurality.

While the incursion from the side of the market is what most analyses of neoliberalism focus on, Marquand also highlights the way in which the public sphere is threatened from the side of the private domain and the logic of private interactions. Marquand identifies two aspects to this threat. The first is what he refers to as the 'revenge of the private', by which he has in mind the protest against the 'hard, demanding, "unnatural" austerities of public duty and public engagement'. This can be seen as the reluctance to engage with the experiment of democracy because it is difficult and demanding – which of course it is. The second aspect touches on the idea of identity politics and is expressed in Marquand's observation that the assumption that 'the private self should be omni-competent and omnipresent' has made deliberative politics of any sort 'virtually impossible'. This resonates with the point I made earlier that engagement with the experiment of democracy not only involves the possibility of the transformation of one's 'issues' – that is, of one's wants – but also of one's identity and one's self.

Q. Can we say that neoliberalism – as a political ideology and political practise – is therefore eroding the public sphere?

GB. I think that's correct. Many commentators have suggested that the decline of the public sphere and the wider 'crisis' in democracy – manifest in such things as low voter turnout in countries where there is no duty to vote, decreased membership of political parties and political organisations and a general decline in interest in democratic politics – is the result of a lack of interest and motivation on the side of citizens. This not only means that citizens are seen as the *cause* of the crisis in democracy – which explains why they are being blamed for it. It also explains the huge investments made in many countries around the world over the past decades in citizenship education on the assumption that we need to create or produce better citizens in order to get better democracy.

This way of thinking fits with a socialisation conception of civic learning where the learning is supposed to produce the good citizen and where, in turn, good citizens are supposed to bring about good democracy. But there is a different reading possible of what is going on, one where the retreat from citizenship is not seen as the *cause* of the crisis in democracy, but rather as its *effect*. By replacing democracy with choice, but letting the logic of the market into the public domain, and by giving up on the idea that democracy is

30   *Gert Biesta et al.*

ultimately about transformation, the possibilities for the enactment of democratic citizenship begin to disappear. While this may look like a process in which citizens are withdrawing from democracy, it is actually a process in which citizens are being 'pushed out' and in which, therefore, the very possibility of democratic citizenship is being pushed out. Rather, therefore, than suggest that we need better citizens in order to get better democracy – which is the argument from the socialisation conception of civic learning – I wish to suggest that we need more and better democracy in order to get better citizens.

Q. What, finally, does that mean for the position of the school? Is it the case, as Hannah Arendt has argued, that the school should remain free from politics?

GB. Here I disagree with Arendt, and I think this partly has to do with the difficulty of thinking about the public sphere and public spaces in terms of qualities of relationships, not as actual locations or institutions. I also think that Arendt has a far too psychological understanding of the difference between children and adults, as she tends to argue that children are simply not capable of living together in plurality, whereas she seems to assume, at least in some of her writings, that adults are. I take the more empirical line here, not only because I see that many adults are not at all able to 'tame' their desires so that living in plurality becomes possible. It is also because I see many children and young people who are perfectly capable of it. And in my more pessimistic moments I actually think that some of the ways in which education is organised in neoliberal societies, for example, with a high emphasis on performance and competition, is eroding children's ability to live together in plurality, because it's sending out the message that such living doesn't really count if you want to be a winner.

Q. Thank you very much.

References

Arendt, H. (1977). What is freedom? In H. Arendt (Ed.), *Between past and future: Eight exercises in political thought* (pp. 143–171). Harmondsworth, UK: Penguin Books.

Bauman, Z. (2000). *Liquid modernity.* Cambridge: Polity Press.

Derrida. J. (1992). Force of law: The 'mystical foundation of authority'. In D. Cornell, M. Rosenfeld and D. Carlson (Eds.), *Deconstruction and the possibility of justice* (pp. 3–67). New York and London: Routledge.

Honneth, A. (1992). *The struggle for recognition: The moral grammar of social conflicts.* Cambridge: Polity Press.

Marquand, D. (2004). *Decline of the public: The hollowing-out of citizenship.* Cambridge: Polity Press.

Mills, C.W. (1959). *The sociological imagination.* Oxford: Oxford University Press.

Mouffe, C. (2000). *The democratic paradox.* London and New York: Verso.

Mouffe, C. (2005). *On the political.* London and New York: Routledge.

Rancière, J. (2003). *The philosopher and his poor.* Durham: Duke University Press.

3 Messy norms and the desire for education

Lena Martinsson

Introduction

The possibility to imagine a society as different from what it is – that it can be organised in another way, that people can understand themselves differently and that one can take part in a societal transformation – could be one definition of political subjectivity.[1] In this chapter, the starting point is Pakistan and the desire and struggle for education for children in the subaltern groups, as well as for children from lower classes. A central question is how political subjectivity can become possible for these children living outside the social and political hegemonies. The object is to discuss three different entrances into this process and the relation between them. I have named the first entrance the pedagogical way, presented by Pakistani educational researchers, teachers, organisations and activists, with a focus on the role of school and education for the emergence of political subjects. The neoliberal intervention in the Pakistani educational assemblage is the second entrance, and the third is the discursive messiness that might enables the emergence of political subjectivity.

As a researcher oriented by postcolonial feminist critique, working with issues on transnational social movements and education as well as with neoliberal normativity reiterated in different ways in different parts of and localities in the world (cf. Rofel 2007; Martinsson 2016; Martinsson and Reimers 2010), I have become deeply frustrated over global rematerialisation of inequalities through education – or through the lack of it. It is part of an ongoing reproduction of class, race and gender that often hinders children from having liveable lives and becoming political subjects. I have also been aware of the translocal and transnational character of education, and the complex and worldwide interdependent relations it emerges from. The schools for subaltern children are, for example, sometimes financed by donors far away. The village in Pakistan I will focus on has a long transnational connection to an exploitative international market. Concepts like children's, women's and workers' rights are reused and transformed all over the world. The reconstruction of a transnational educating middle class is valid in Sweden as well as in Pakistan, and the neoliberal normativity that I will come back to soon is very prevalent and normalised in the Swedish school system today as it is in Pakistan (Ball 2012, 2013; Siddiqui 2012). In spite of this, I will also address the importance of locality and place. Norms will always be transformed in relation to other norms and materialities. The Pakistani situation,

32 *Lena Martinsson*

as well as the situation in the village that I will focus later in this chapter, reflects the emergence of different space-specific normative materialities which condition any transformation. I will therefore use the concept of 'assemblage', meaning an affective concentration of potential changing norms, materialities (bodies, house, economies), discourses etc. in order to understand places like the village, which can be understood as a special entanglement of inhabitants, different economic principles, norms and beliefs. Looking at the village as an entanglement also makes it possible to understand how norms and materialities can affect each other in a non-linear way. The entanglements are understood as performative, they do something. Finally, of importance for this chapter is that instead of understanding the complexity of identities and subjectivities as equal to several different positions, such as woman, white, working class and homosexual, I understand the ongoing emergence of identity and subjectivity also as an entanglement where conditional norms and discourses, material conditions, body and so forth continuously affect and merge into or confront and thereby affect each other in ways that are far from predictable. My thesis is that it is in these frictions, where a person or a group is addressed in different and contradictory ways, that political subjectivity can emerge (cf. Butler 2015; Barad, 2007; Mouffe 2013; Puhar 2007).

The material used in this chapter consists principally of interviews and participant observations from Pakistan. I have regularly visited Pakistan since 2006, after 2009 approximately once a year. I have conducted interviews both in the countryside and in cities, with activists and especially with feminists or women taking part in different women's movements, with schoolchildren, parents and teachers. I have participated in meetings, met with teachers and listened to lectures both in rural villages and at universities. I have worked as a guest researcher at Lahore College for Women University. Together with my colleague Erika Alm, I have also conducted interviews with journalists, lawyers, writers and transgender activists.

The outline

I will begin with a brief overview of important critiques of the education available to subaltern children and children from the lower classes. The next section focuses on educational interventions which aim to change conditions for people living in difficult circumstances in locations where education for the children is of low quality or nonexistent. I consider the teachers, researchers and activists focused on in this section to be important political subjects. I categorise three of these interventions with their goal of educating children to become reflexive citizens and political subjects as critically important.

I find the fourth, the neoliberal, 'solution' strongly problematic and a good example of transnational depoliticising normativity. The following section of the text, which I consider the most important, focuses on the rural Pakistani village already mentioned, where different norms and normative materialities in a contradictory and affective way merge into or challenge each other. I try to understand what this messiness can mean for the possibility of the emergence of subjectivity, especially political subjectivity.

Thinking outside the box

Khadim Hussain (2012) and Shahid Siddiqui (2012, 2014), two educational researchers of particular importance for this chapter, strongly criticise the Pakistani educational system for not teaching children who attend government or public schools, primarily children in the lower classes, to think critically – to think outside the box. Hussain even asks what shapes the behaviours and creates a 'culture of silence'. Gayatri Chakravorty Spivak has stressed that low-quality educations for the subaltern children reproduce the class society over and over again. She especially stresses that some classes with access to aesthetic education have opportunities to be trained in advanced thinking that enables them to imagine something different (Spivak 2008, 2012). Siddiqui especially addresses the fact that NGO schools and other donor agencies that are oriented to these children often tend to focus on vocational education, while social studies and humanities are pushed back (Siddiqui 2012). The ambition to provide vocational training without also offering education in social studies and humanities is strong internationally and problematic because it assumes that political knowledge is not necessary. The thinking is that, if people just learn skills and get jobs, the society will be transformed by itself.[2] It is a discourse that does not encourage political subjectivity and critical thinking among the most exposed, and it needs therefore to be challenged. Or as Spivak expresses it, with reference to Gramsci:

> If we want to 'change the world', alter-globalism must think of the education of the disenfranchised into disinterest in a double bind with the interest of class struggle: 'democracy . . . cannot mean merely that an unskilled worker can become skilled,' writes Gramsci. 'It must mean that every 'citizen' can 'govern' and that society places him, even if only abstractly, in a general condition to achieve this'.
>
> (Spivak 2012, p. 8)

A school system, like the one in Pakistan, is therefore a performative part of an extreme national as well as international class system. And it is important to remember that, in Pakistan, there are figures estimating that anywhere from 5 million to 25 million children don't go to school at all.[3]

While the Pakistani state doesn't recognise these children who don't get a good enough education, or any education at all, as citizens with rights, I have noticed many national and international interventions into this school situation. There are neoliberal international ventures, donations from Saudi Arabia and ventures from Pakistani women's movements. There are human rights organisations and different sorts of welfare NGOs that not infrequently get support from the Pakistani state and from the regional governments. Many NGOs of different kinds, of course, also receive funding from abroad. To let NGOs, whether they do a good job or not, be responsible for schools for precarious and subaltern children is of course a problematic and short-sighted solution, very much in line with how these children are positioned and handled as a group outside the society. NGOs cannot be institutionalised, they are project-oriented and the unwillingness to

34 *Lena Martinsson*

change the situation politically for this huge group of children becomes evident. However, the broad interest in education shows the political role education is understood to have in a country such as Pakistan. For some it becomes a way to transform society, to challenge class society and patriarchal hegemonies, or just to give precarious children more options (Siddiqui 2012).

The many discourses on precarious and subaltern children as objects for different interventions like the ones just mentioned sometimes worry me for quite another reason, and I would therefore like to pause for a moment before I continue my discussion. I have noticed that when the poor and uneducated are discussed and presented among, for example, researchers or in aid discourses (Goyder et al. 2014), it is nearly impossible to understand them as subjects and certainly not as political subjects. School education often becomes a precondition in these discussions for individual as well as collective political subjectivity to emerge. Without school education, it seems impossible to act. Some movements among the poor, such as Ekta Parishad in India, challenge this quite dominant discourse of the importance of school education for being able to act politically.[4] Without reflections like these, the necessary critique against the poor-quality, class-, race- and gender-(re)producing education risks further stabilising the notion of the poor dehumanised mass at the same time as it recentres the inter/national middle class as those who shall bring about change and who shall be the political subjects. A radical strategy for change needs a responsible middle class, prepared to struggle for equality and better school education for all children, and it also needs, paradoxically, to decentre itself in order to make it possible for other subjectivities to emerge. While education that is good enough to challenge processes of undemocratic normalisations like the ones just mentioned is a fundamental right, it is important not to reproduce the idea of the silent mass by making education into a rescuing power without context. It is of course as important, when trying to overcome this problem, not to reproduce a positive subaltern essentialism (Spivak 2008). However, if the view that education is a prerequisite for subjectivity, and for political subjectivity, is not challenged, there is a risk of further normalising the uneducated as, at best objects for the educated middle class to deal with, or at worst, as a hopeless mass that cannot be helped.

Educational interventions

The problem of exposed children not being educated in critical thinking, described by Hussain, Siddiqui and Spivak, is well known. Many pedagogues, researchers and activists challenge this double inequality, and organisations and other forces have tried through different means to transform education. Research and school material are produced, and new schools are started and teacher training arranged. Campaigns as well as demonstrations are organised. Spivak herself has been running schools, and she claims that those who are engaged in educating subaltern groups on subjects such as human rights need to learn from below and thereby challenge their own superiority and the class system (2008). Simorgh, a feminist resource and publication organisation in Lahore, is another example. Simorgh was once funded by a group of teachers, and Neelham Hussain, Simorgh's executive coordinator, states that this is why education has become so important for the organisation. N. Hussain is a famous feminist, writer, literature researcher and teacher, with deep knowledge of the Pakistani state (Hussain 2004; Hussain et al. 1997, 2005). She and the organisation work with teacher training and stress the need for teachers to connect to the children's own lives and languages. In her education of teachers, N. Hussain strongly questions the superior attitudes held by teachers towards the children. N. Hussain, and Simorgh, further stresses the need to develop school material on social sciences and the importance of learning from children. One example of how they work is that they make connections between the Sufi tradition or other old cultural heritage stories, stories that the pupils are familiar with, and they let these stories work as connections to issues such as human rights. For Simorgh and N. Hussain, it has always been important to start with the children and bring them into the development of the textbooks.[5]

The Bonded Labour Liberation Front Society (BLLFS) is the next example. The organisation was started by a group of former bonded labourers, or debt slaves, together with middle-class persons who had worked in trade unions. Those who themselves had experienced bonded labour were illiterate and without school education, but they knew about resistance and the struggle for change. The organisation was established with the aim of freeing other bonded labourers and also to end slavery through education. After some years, the organisation received support from a newly funded Swedish organisation, an organisation I joined myself many years later. Together, they applied for money from the Swedish state to start and develop schools for the children of bonded labourers. From the start it was important to develop a school system that aimed to develop confident children who are not easily exploited, who are able to work cooperatively with others and are comfortable with public speaking. It was forbidden for the teachers to punish pupils by hitting them. The school also organised children's committees, mothers' as well as fathers' committees.

Khadim Hussain, the researcher cited above, is also director for the Baacha Khan Trust Educational Foundation (BKTEF) (2015). The BKTEF is the last example I want to discuss. As a researcher and director, K. Hussain is not only critical towards the educational system, he also criticises the impact the colonial system has had on education. In his discussions with principals and teachers, he stresses the importance of pluralism, equality, critical creative and political thinking and the need for social and political studies (Baacha Khan Trust Educational Foundation 2015). In mail correspondence, K. Hussain told me that he was engaged at the BKTEF because he thinks it is 'important to develop an alternative model of education and then lobby for injecting it into the public education sector'. He also told me that BKTEF wants 'to build a system of education that develops the students' critical and analytical thinking, problem-solving and social skills'. He wants to include literary and artistic subjects as well as training in indigenous marketable skills, and to establish a community-based system of education. He and the organisation want change – change through education. From my perspective, the organisation seems impressive. It has established 15 community-based schools where more than 5,000 students are enrolled, and there are 300 full-time staff in 10 districts of the region Khyber-Pakhtunkhwa and Federally

36 *Lena Martinsson*

Administered Tribal Areas (FATA) in the northwest part of Pakistan. The aim is 'to empower the underserved communities by providing them free and subsidised quality educational services'. They also want to '[empower] women by educating and involving them in decision-making processes at all levels'.

The desire for education and the outspoken ambition to let the children and students become political subjects, or at least have opportunities to 'govern', is salient for the organisations. It has been an aim for the poor groups to be able, as N. Hussain from Simorgh said, 'to think for themselves; I can't decide what they shall think, they might join the Talibans, I can't predict that'. In other words, her approach to teaching is an example on what Biesta has described as the importance of taking a risk. Education is a risk. One cannot predict what will come out of it (Biesta 2006). What she is hinting at might be described as becoming a political subject, getting opportunities through fantasy work, aesthetic work, to imagine other possibilities, other possible societies and identities – to be open to the unpredictable. K. Hussain is focusing on the same matter, the ambition to make another type of society possible. Like N. Hussain, he also stresses the importance of knowledge that reaches beyond the colonial influence, a connection between the indigenous history of the place and critical thinking. Simorgh, BKTEF and BLLFS are, as collective organisations, political subjects that have emerged in a crossroad of a course of events, norms and transformations. Simorgh is, for example, part of a feminist movement that started when General Zia became dictator in Pakistan during the 1980s and women became interpellated in a very oppressive way that became impossible for many to identify with. Women's rise against the state during this period has been thoroughly discussed in a book edited by Nighat Khan (2004).

Due to a lack of funding, many interventions like the ones just described in Pakistani schools have been withdrawn. There are still many similar ventures like these going on, but without the recognition of a state, they become more or less dependent on support from donors, states abroad or volunteers. Some of the examples presented above are actively searching for money. Schools like these are, of course, vulnerable. The Swedish state, the former donor to the BLLFS project, cut the funds with the argument that the Pakistani nation should pay for its own schools. One nation interpellates, or expects action from, another. The Simorgh project, which was also internationally financed, always suffered from a lack of funds, but they were shut out from schools and teacher education after the school bombing in Islamabad in 2014. To turn away from the state, 'to give it up' as one informant expressed it, is not the only way of handling the situation, however. The vision of the welfare state that recognises and protects all its citizens is a global discourse and as such, it is also articulated in the significant and well-known organisation Human Rights Commission Pakistan (HRCP).[6] They are struggling to develop democracy, and as the leader IA Rehman stresses, they approach the state as if this state worked as a welfare state would work.[7] The HRCP demands education, demonstrates the country's shortcomings in the area of human rights and comes with expectations for action.

A way of framing these different ventures is to understand them as entanglements of organisations, academia and debates that connect through a joint transnational way of understanding the problem of lack of education. However, it is also a joint and frictional way of trying to do the work states don't do. They both turn away from the state and interpellate it, and they try to do what they think a welfare state should have done: offer critical education.

In the next section, I will focus on another transnational intervention into the educational system, the neoliberal one: it is a venture without the double bind between education and class struggle.

Neoliberal interventions

In the West, neoliberalism is usually understood as an economic normativity that deconstructs welfare societies with institutions such as comprehensive schools and public health care systems. Under neoliberalism, these institutions become part of the market, which means that the institutions – education in this case – become customer-oriented. Education is turned into a commodity, teachers become sellers and parents and students become customers (Ball 2012; Biesta 2006, 2009; Harvey 2009). This description of neoliberalism has relevance in nations that have had a welfare state with a strong ideology of becoming an equal national community, which can then be deconstructed. Sweden has this background. Pakistan has not. But the neoliberal normativity is salient even in Pakistan. It points to the market as the solution to different national problems, such as poverty, gender inequality and environmental pollution. The market becomes the arena for change, and political struggle seems unnecessary. With the neoliberal normativity follows the subject position, telling people what to do and how to understand themselves: they should be strong individuals, competitive, entrepreneurial and not interested in political life. So even though Pakistan has never had a welfare society, the neoliberal discourse with its questioning of the politically driven welfare society based on collective resources and with a belief in the central role of the market is a discourse that is repeated and translated locally as well as globally (Siddiqui 2012).

An example of how neoliberal normativity (cf. Brown 2015) works in Pakistan as well as in Sweden and worldwide is the corporate social responsibility (CSR) network. It is organised as a loose affiliation of transnational consultancy businesses (for example, Sustainia) and national or transnational networks such as CSR Sweden or CSR Pakistan. In 2009, the latter published the book *CSR Pakistan* (Mian 2009), presenting neoliberal development projects in the country. The message is that Pakistan can become a successful neoliberal place and market, and the poor youth can then be a productive resource. In the book, companies such as English Biscuit Manufactures, Hiopak, TetraPak, Indus Motor Company and Shell Pakistan present their CSR ventures.

When Pakistan is understood through this neoliberal discourse, the political goal becomes intertwined with the economic one. The focus is on creating a market and on creating customers who can 'think for themselves' instead of being 'fundamentalists' because this is important for the market. The overall goal is to accomplish a good environment for entrepreneurship. *CSR Pakistan* incites leaders and business owners as well as other entrepreneurs to be responsible, and

38   *Lena Martinsson*

the introductory pages in the book deal with the extensive role of business for societal change and for nation building. The reason for taking responsibility for the country and its exposed children is that the profits will grow as well as the number of customers if these people become customers. There exists a commodity market, which can grow considerably (Mian 2009). The text presents a vision of how to build a new society:

> For the business to play a productive role in expediting development and progress, political and economic stability is a necessity. Without peace and political will of the government, the business will not be able to do enough to reduce rising poverty and lack of education in the urban and rural communities. An environment conducive for business and investment is essential for companies to operate efficiently, and make a difference in the lives of their employees and local communities.
>
> (Mian 2009, p. 16)

Business, in this quote, is identified and understood as a force for change: it will reduce the rising poverty and address the lack of education. The condition is that the government will organise peace and stability and thereby produce a good environment that encourages entrepreneurship. As with other CSR organisations, CSR Pakistan stresses that society actors – government, civil society, donors and the media – need to join forces in order to find the strength to push the process forward (Mian 2009).[8] In this sense, they promote the idea of a cohesive society, wherein the market is good for everyone. Working together, they will resist the dangerous forces: terrorism and fundamentalism (Mian 2009). There appear to be two camps: the neoliberal consensus on the one hand, and fundamentalism/terrorism on the other. No further political options are recognised.

In the preface of the book on CSR in Pakistan, it is said that Pakistan has the potential to become an economic power in South Asia. The country will use 'the greatest resource . . . the young and energetic people' in an efficient and effective way. Half of the population is under 25 years old. The pictures in the book emphasise 'youth' as an important subject. The youths are presented as a strong collective, even if it is divided along gender lines. This collective is expected to be set in motion. The company Shell states that they educate the young people to become entrepreneurs because as entrepreneurs, they will be able to 'help themselves' (Mian 2009, p. 89 f.). It is an individual approach, an interpellation, and it sends a message that no one else will help – that it is up to each individual to look out for him – or herself (cf. Brown 2015).

A photograph of several women is combined with a text about what would make female entrepreneurship possible. Engineering, science and entrepreneurship are in focus and are the only professional specialisations mentioned (see, e.g., Mian 2009, pp. 57, 58, 68, 81, 83). The education is limited to what Biesta calls qualification for careers and socialisation into a market economic thinking. The importance of political subjectivity that would make it possible for the students to develop new or different political visions and to think in different ways is not discussed or visualised. The neoliberal organisation seems to be the one and only that matter. The education proposed is not designed to make political agency or subjectivity possible. It is seen as the natural basis for creating human capital and a well-functioning neoliberal society (cf. Biesta 2006, 2014; Hussain 2012). A vision of Pakistan beyond the political is created. In a society where the struggle for a better democracy is very harsh, this neoliberal normativity fits well. Chantal Mouffe warned about this depoliticising trend when she observed it in the West. It is about a desire to eliminate political situations with clear antagonistic positions in order to create consensus (2005). It is a dangerous road, she writes, and she stresses the importance of encouraging agonistic positions which recognise the existence of other alternatives and the ongoing conflict between them, and of making the conflicts visible. In other words, it might be said that she stresses the importance of an education that challenges an idea of a cohesive society.

In the book *Spaces of Global Capitalism*, the geographer David Harvey notes that the neoliberal state does not take on the responsibility for education (2009, p. 28). I would rather say that the neoliberal discourse materialises a state with limited subjectivity. It is a product. The state should, due to neoliberal discourse, just have one for the business supporting function. The CSR example shows the effect this neoliberal normativity has on how education is understood in a limited way, as a resource for the market.

Messiness

So far, I have discussed how school and good education are supposed to change society, in some cases making the emergence of political subjectivity possible. In this section, I will discuss how political subjectivity can emerge in a messy assemblage which school is plugged into, becoming one of many, maybe frictional, parts of an entanglement. I will therefore not enter into the classroom in this section, nor interest myself in different pedagogical aims. Instead, I will stay outside the classroom in a Pakistani village, where many different norms or discourses are reiterated, transformed together with a plurality of normative effects and appeals. It is not the teachers who are in focus here, trying to teach pupils to think for themselves, 'outside the box', or teaching aesthetics. Instead, it is the assemblage of frictional normative and discursive materialities that are in focus (Barad 2007; Butler 2015). What I want to discuss in this section is how contradictory entanglements of discourses, norms and normative materialities where the school is plugged in can be a condition for political subjectivity, and thereby antagonism, to emerge (Laclau and Mouffe 1985).

Feudal mindset

Several activists and representatives of educational institutions that I have sought out and interviewed in Pakistan underline the importance of challenging 'the feudal mindset' and 'feudal principles' that they see as widespread in the country, a description that is also underlined and discussed by researchers (Shaikh 2009; cf. Hussain 2012). One example of the feudal order is the existence of debt slaves, who are strongly exploited and subordinated by landlords and owners of

40   *Lena Martinsson*

brick kilns and looms, for example. This illegal but very much working system normalises for those who are exploited a life without politics, without any sort of subjectivity beyond that as a bonded labourer. In my own studies in Pakistan, I have also observed how the feudal discourse is repeated in and articulated with colonial discourses as well as with contemporary global discourses on market economy and neoliberal normativity. Today, carpets are tied in the Thar Desert, often by debt slaves and often by children. These children are primarily understood and expected to act as a source of income or as workers rather than as, for example, schoolchildren, children at play or as a possible force for societal changes. The carpets are most often sold at foreign markets (Soomro et al. 2009); they are seldom sold in the Pakistani market. The transnational market has therefore had an impact on these villages for a very long time. However, the debt slaves, the child labourers, have never been recognised as true members of a capitalist society. They have just been positioned as producers, not as employees with rights nor as consumers in this transnational sphere. And, of course, they have not been recognised as equal human beings, but as bodies to be exploited.

However, different discourses are also frictional, and even in situations like these, political subjectivity and antagonism or uncertainty can emerge. I want to focus on how the feudal and neoliberal discourses are reiterated in a village where a quite radical and progressive school has been plugged in. This school has been run by the Pakistani anti-slavery organisation BLLFS, mentioned earlier, with financial support from the Swedish government. The slogan for this school is: 'Struggle against slavery through education'. As I mentioned earlier, the conviction that slavery could be abolished through education was strong in BLLFS. After 10 years, the school received no more funds from the Swedish government far away from the village. It was just a project, and projects end. NGOs are fragile constructions, but while most of these schools in the desert were closed, the school in this village was taken over and run by the parents themselves. The teacher, who was paid very little, continued to go for training organised by the organisation that had started the school. One way of describing it is that the school was or had been plugged into a feudal context with transnational connections.

Sometime before my visit to the village, an NGO had arrived, offering microloans to the villagers. The idea was for them to start small businesses and let the market solve the problem of poverty in the region. The discourse on entrepreneurship was also evident in the desert. I noticed signs where people identified themselves as entrepreneurs, and I met some women who had things to sell in this village with a very small amount of capital. One of them gave me a candy from the tray of sweets that was her store. Even though I am really worried about what a neoliberal-oriented school could do in villages like these, or to education around the globe (the neoliberal ignorance for political and democratic education, and the unconcern to teach pupils to think in critical and non-predictable ways is highly problematic), I did notice that these neoliberal interventions made new positions of subjectivity possible, at least for a while. With the NGO intervention, some of the villagers were interpellated as entrepreneurs and as possible consumers. It became a new way of acting. I do not assume that this marketisation will solve the problems of this village, but it was an economic intervention in the village, offering other more or less possible positions and also other ways of understanding economy. It might have made the former, one and only, economic position less given. My point is not that there are no problems with the neoliberal NGOs, or any other NGOs. It is important for me to underline that there are problems with the ongoing 'NGOisation': it risks transforming political movements into relationships between employers and employees, and it is not the result of democratic processes. NGOs are not a solution. However, my point here is to decentre their importance, and underline that they actually accomplish things in a way that might not have been the stated aim. In this example, they might have failed to solve the problem of poverty through marketisation. But the neoliberal intervention, interpellating some as entrepreneurs and thereby also others as consumers, offered not only alternative ways for people to understand themselves, it was a contradictory interpellation to the way people had been able to understand themselves in a feudal normativity, as bonded labourers. It offered different and contradictory interpellations and thereby different subject positions (Mouffe 2013), and thus also possible contradictory ideas about other ways of acting and being.

Women become political subjects

The women in the village had recently heard about the existence of women's rights. It was, one might say, another sort of norm that was merged into the entanglement of the village. I am not sure how they got the information: some of them told me that they had first understood that the men had rights, and then after that the children and themselves. Maybe it was the children who had taught them about women's rights, or an NGO. I don't know. But in the same village as feudal and patriarchal mindsets were repeated, where the level of illiteracy was high among the adults, there were also discourses on human rights, workers' rights, women's rights and, not least, children's rights, reiterated and transformed into everyday lives. It was another way of being addressed: you are someone, you have rights too. When I interviewed women about what they thought when they learned that they had rights, several told me that it changed their lives or it meant a lot to them. It is, of course, possible to criticise these interventions and assert that these groups should find out by themselves how to challenge the system and do it in their own way (Tsing 2005). However, the discourses on human rights cannot be owned by just some groups of people who then get to decide who should and should not learn about them. In this case, they certainly offered another possible way for individuals to understand themselves. And again, the most important effect could have been the frictional relation between local, national and international norms and structures.

Some of the women had also joined a female network and they had started to have meetings. They were tired of patriarchy, loans and poverty, and also of NGOs coming and going. They saw the downside of the shortage of funds that the Simorgh organisation and BLLFS struggled with. They were, of course, also angry about not getting any support, health care, schools for their children or

42 Lena Martinsson

protection from the government. They knew they had rights and that these rights weren't being recognised by the state. There was also an expectation on the NGOs to recognise their rights. But the NGOs could not be entirely trusted: they came to stay for a while and then disappeared. NGOs, which are project-oriented and in many ways depend on voluntary work and engagement, can never be expected to be the ones to recognise people's rights; they cannot be responsible for providing protection etc. The village was, subaltern, placed outside the social and political hegemony, and in that way not fully part of transnational or Pakistani infrastructural network; it was as if they didn't belong, not counted among the Pakistani people (cf. Spivak 1988, 2008; Butler 2015).

When I visited the village I stayed with Rakhi, a woman I had met on some female network meetings. She is a strong force for change in the village. She and the other women in this village said that one thing they had learned from the NGOs, including from the new one that visited the village when I was there, was to have meetings. They constructed public places. One way of describing this is to say that they recognised themselves not only as subjects but also as a collective: they lived among each other, they cohabited and even if they hadn't chosen each other, they had discovered each other and they became a political group. The women had commenced meeting across the religious borders in the village in order to, as they said, 'strengthen ourselves and the whole community'. The challenging of borders between different religions is something I have noticed at other meetings as well. In BLLFS, they start every meeting with a prayer connected to each religion represented in the group. Living side by side with other religions has a long tradition in the subcontinent even after 1947, when Pakistan become a Muslim state and made the other religions into minorities.

The group of women struggled for the school, which was understood as being of huge importance not only for each child, but also for the future of the village. They had taken it over after the NGO that started it left. They built an infrastructure and strengthened the interdependence in the village. The women indicated that they had high hopes for the school and that it would help to bring changes in the village. The school was therefore in itself affecting the community and created a challenging mess, an idea about other sorts of possible lives, for producing imaginations. Even here, the idea of school as something that would bring about change was repeated. The group of women had also started to save money. Now they were not as dependent as before and would not need to borrow from the landlord or seek support from an NGO if someone needed health care, for example.

It is also worth noting, once again, that discourses do not appear in order, one after the other. They cannot be understood as a development chain, and they need not be consistent. They are entangled with each other in both stabilising and frictional ways (cf. Boatca 2012; Barad 2007; Hussain 2004; Laclau and Mouffe 1985). The simultaneous and parallel articulation of the material discourses showed the villagers that lives and communities can be organised in different ways, and they therefore serve as a condition for a politic or antagonistic situation to emerge. It is also important to be aware that these different normativities are material; the neoliberal micro-credit program was based on a global normative principle. When reiterated in the village, it was one thing. It became something else when it was reiterated or plugged in, for example, in a Swedish suburb. And when neoliberal normativity is reiterated in different economic hegemony, its effects are not totally predictable. The feudal order was another materiality, creating positions of landlords and bonded labourers, and third was the school, wanting to challenge the feudal class system. To challenge this system was a political ambition that actually was materialised through the school, through the pupils learning to read, count and ask questions. The different norms were all material, and they also challenged each other. They became frictional and produced contradictory interpellations, contradictory talks about possible lives, about possible societies (Mouffe 2013). There were different ways for individuals to understand themselves, the community and the future. I want to point out these different discursive educational economic contexts to clarify the political dimension that is in them and how 'education', and also the understandings and creations of children's and parents' subjectivity and imagined political roles, might be produced. In the next section, I will focus on the complex and partly contradictory subjectivities in the same individual.

One child, many positions

There was an ongoing discussion in the village, both among children and adults, concerning what a child was supposed to be and how a child was to act. Was a child a source of income to repay loans, or should the young ones be understood as schoolchildren that will contribute to social change and thereby abolish slavery or would they maybe become entrepreneurs? Even the children themselves were part of these ongoing discussions, and they had been so for quite a long time. I interviewed Kewal, today a young man, who had experienced different phases, ideologies and interventions in the village. When Kewal was a small child, his father had to, due to sickness in the family, take a loan from an owner of a loom. As an illiterate loan taker, the father was not protected against the conditions of the loan the owner set up. Kewal became therefore the one who had to pay off a never-ending loan. He became a bonded labourer, a debt slave. He sat and worked at the loom, producing carpets that would be sold far away. He told me when we talked about it that he thought that that was life. He didn't think that school was for boys like him. Or, to put it in another way, he was, as Butler might have described it, interpellated or talked to and thereby he understood himself as a debt slave who had to work. He had to identify himself with that position. But, and this is important to stress, Kewal was never equated with the position of debt slave. It is impossible to just identify with and be subjected to one normative position. There are always different norms, and they can be contradictory. Kewal did get a lot of knowledge and education from his family. He learned how to take care of cattle, how to cook food and take care of his siblings. This was important knowledge that also must be understood as some types of interpellations, addressing what life should be and what it is to be responsible. The work he did demanded activity and required him to make decisions.

Kewal had also learned to paint from his parents, and they had learned from their parents. Rakhi's house was decorated with flowers, camels and peacocks

44 *Lena Martinsson*

painted by Kewal. It had not been a way to earn money, Kewal told me, it was just for fun and because it was beautiful. He had been drawing and painting not only in his own village but also in others, for example, painting and decorating homes in preparation for wedding celebrations, as is the custom.

Kewal's life in the village was more than slavery, and his identity was more than that of a child labourer. When I listened to Kewal and looked at his paintings, it became clear to me that in Kewal's village there are many contradictions and activities that could challenge the feudal and patriarchal order (cf. Laclau and Mouffe 1985). So when the anti-slavery school was placed in the village, Kewal had already experienced different ways of life, used different skills and held different positions. But still, when the school started and Kewal was called to attend, he suddenly understood, he told me, that life could be something very different. He was talked to in a new way and thereby displaced.

Kewal also told me that the schoolchildren, and the children's committee, had had the role of persuading reluctant parents to let their children go to school and of informing the parents of the importance of allowing their children to be educated. This activity was a way to challenge, to disidentify with, the position of the working child and try to convince the parents of this as well. Many different norms interrupted each other. Identity as well as the question of how to act became a frictional emergence. Kewal told me that these committees, when he was young, also collected and saved money for the children living in difficult circumstances. He still thinks the work of the children's committees was a very good thing. 'We want to rebuild that again', he said to me when we met some years after he had left school for college. What Kewal was addressing was how the pupils had the role of getting the other children out of the home, away from work, and it may also say something about how they were interpellated, as changers, as individuals who could criticise the exploitive system and even the adults. The children became transformative subjects, able to think about themselves in different ways and to discover that they could, and were supposed to, persuade the adults (cf. Sundhall 2014). Saba Mahmood writes in her book *Politics of Piety* 'that practises may also be undertaken on a smaller scale wherein people teach themselves to inhabit a different kind of body, sensibility, aesthetics, or argumentative form' (2012, p. xiii). The activities in the school, and maybe also the skills of painting and being responsible, exemplify how different kinds of bodies can become possible.

Kewal himself pointed out that it is not possible to foresee what is going to happen. He had wanted to take part in the struggle for change, and he wanted to get an education, but his brothers didn't share that desire. They wanted to take care of the cattle, and that was also fine, said Kewal. The brothers, just like Kewal, also understood themselves from different discourses and normative materialities, and it cannot be predicted what subjectivity will emerge (Mouffe 1992).

The last interview I did with Kewal was in a bigger city, many hours away from his home village. Kewal had started in college and lived in the house of one of the leaders of the anti-slavery organisation. Outside the window we could see and hear people living in a camp, in small shelters built of paper, boards, fabric and lumber. Kewal explained to me that the children we saw from the window did not go to school; he lifted his hand and pointed towards the window, saying, 'I was one of them, I lived under the same conditions. It could have been me'. In this sentence, Kewal came back to two different things that I think are of special importance. He told me that it is possible to inhabit another sort of body: as Mahmood expressed it, you can become someone else and the place you live can be different. It is a political statement. But Kewal also identified himself with the children, thereby recognising them as something more than a problematic subaltern mass.

In Chapter 2 of this book, Biesta says that it is not possible to separate civil learning from other types of learning: they are connected. The story Kewal tells says that, in him, different concurring systems about how to understand the child crossed, in his life and in the village. Kewal underlined in an interview that it was so important that the schools educate the children not only in the different subjects, but also about other things – 'about rights'. For him, as for so many others, hearing about rights had been of great importance. When I hear this, the words of K. Hussain, N. Hussain and G.C. Spivak have a special resonance. At the same time, it is too easy to say that it was enough simply to know about rights. What Kewal's story conveys is not just that he has learned about the existence of human rights and women's and children's rights. What the story tells is that these discourses on rights have, through contradictory interpellations, displaced him and thereby created possible different positions and possible desires for another life for himself and for the village. Kewal is optimistic when he talks about his own village. He even states that the landlord system has improved, that the people 'have learned that they are human beings', and that 'it is better now'. Also, the girls are educated, they have finished their education 'with good remarks', 'educated women have knowledge about democracy' and 'the uneducated women (in other villages) don't know about their rights'. Kewal continues by stating that 'education is most important; the village is different through education'.

At the same time, during the same interview, Kewal continued to express criticism against the exploitive order he could see around him in the bigger city he lives in now. It is an order that makes it possible for some to even buy their college certificates instead of earning them. He talked, as so many others have, about the problematic corruption that makes it so difficult for poor people to have the same opportunities for higher education as the wealthy. I think that Kewal has made an important analysis here, showing that he and other poor students are exposed to an inadequate system and to a state that fail to recognise them through recognising their rights and that fail to protect them, even when they have reached college. The village might have changed, but Kewal is still exposed to a societal system of precarisation. It is a subordination that could give rise to antagonism and maybe more outspoken political struggle for change (cf. Mouffe 2013).

On pluralism and messiness: a summary

In this chapter, conditions for political subjectivity have been scrutinised. I started by discussing pedagogical ambitions to teach students how to become political subjects. As a contrast to these interventions, neoliberal interventions and their depoliticising force were focused on. I then changed perspectives, and instead of thinking about how to teach students to become political subjects, I elaborated on how political subjectivity can emerge in a messy situation full of different frictional norms, practises, normative materialities and discourses. With help from Chantal Mouffe's concept of contradictory interpellation (Mouffe 2013), I discussed how women and children in a village were interpellated in many different ways, which made it possible for them to become aware that life could be otherwise: society could be different, and the children can have another future. The role of the school as a place where people can learn about human rights and democracy is of course important. But, what I have wanted to emphasise in this section has been something else: the role of the school offered another interpellation and become frictional in the context of the village. It articulated through its existence another story about life and society. Neoliberalism, as it appeared in the village, was not discussed as a problematic force that hindered the political. Instead, it was understood as a normative force producing subject positions that differed from the ones produced by the old colonial and feudal norms and normative materialities. In the same way, norms on rights were plugged into a feudal and colonial order. The messiness made it possible to challenge any stable order and to discuss other ways of life.

But there are also risks with messiness. Even if it is apparent that different discourses can create frictional relationships with each other and thereby question different sorts of hegemonies, allowing for the emergence of 'better democracies', other emergences are also possible. The neoliberal discourse might very well be articulated with and be strengthened by the content of a feudal one, reiterating the latter's total neglect of politics, in a neoliberal frame. People who have not had any chance to develop political subjectivity, who have never been interpellated as political agents, can of course recognise, and feel at home in, a neoliberal normativity that just wants people to follow what is best for the market, to become neoliberal subjects. The non-recognition of the political is something that is significant in both the neoliberal and the feudal normativity. It is a problematic risk, which shows that it is necessary to actually keep the messiness alive as a reality and as a story.

What is said and done in classrooms is, of course, utterly important. I believe, inspired by Takayama in this book, that it is possible to discuss the messiness just described in the classrooms context as well. Different norms concerning how society, communities or families can be organised and how personal lives can be lived can challenge hegemonies and make the importance of the political clear at the same time as plurality can be supported and normalised. Thereby, not only the messiness in itself can be an important part in an ongoing emergence of a 'better' democracy, the story or discussion about this messiness can also be important. It can be possible to understand more about the complex interdependence between people, and between people and norms and materialities, and to see these complexities as forms of political access. Again, this messy plurality can open up for other possible societies and assembled identities, but as N. Hussain so strongly noted, there is of course no safe end. But the risk we need to take is, at the same time, unavoidable.

Notes

1 This chapter is built on the work in two research projects, 'Dreaming of Change' and 'Class in Neoliberal Education', both funded by the Swedish Research Council. I especially want to thank Kewal and Reikhi: without you, this text would not have been possible.
2 See, for example, *Nyhetsbrevet Bllf Sweden* 2016:1, www.Bllf.se.
3 According to Human Rights Commission Pakistan (HRCP 2014), over 5 million children don't go to school at all, while Alif Ailaan's corresponding figures are 25 million children out of school (http://www.alifailaan.pk/).
4 Lecture and interview with PW Rajagopal, October 2015.
5 Look, for example, at *Kaleidoscope 1–5.*
6 HRCP; http://www.hrcp-web.org
7 Interview, November 2015.
8 See, for example, http://www.sustainia.me

References

Baacha Khan Trust Educational Foundation (2015). Leadership Fellowship Seminar, Accessed online, 10 March 2016. Available at: http://bkefoundation.org/index. php?option=com_content&view=article&id=351:leadership-fellowship-seminar&catid=3:newsflash

Ball, S.J. (2012). *Global education.* New York: Routledge.

Ball, S.J. (2013). *Foucault, power, and education.* London: Routledge.

Barad, K. (2007). *Meeting the universe halfway: Quantum physics and the entanglement of matter and meaning.* Durham: Duke University Press.

Biesta, G. (2006). *Beyond learning: Democratic education for a human future.* Boulder, CO: Paradigm Publisher.

Biesta, G. (2009). *Good education in an age of measurement: Ethics, politics, democracy.* Boulder, CO: Paradigm Publisher.

Biesta, G. (2014). *The beautiful risk of education.* Boulder, CO: Paradigm Publishers.

Boatca, M. (2012). De många icke-väst [The many non-Western]. *Fronesis.* 38–39: 96–115.

Brown, W. (2015). *Undoing the demos: Neoliberalism's stealth the revolution.* New York: Zone Books.

Butler, J. (2015). *Notes toward a performative theory of assembling.* London: Harvard University Press.

Goyder, H., Raoof, S., Quasmi, M. and Haider, M.N. (2014). *Pakistan country report.* Stockholm: Sipu.

Harvey, D. (2009). *Spaces of global capitalism: A theory of uneven geographical development.* London: Verso.

HRCP. (2014). *State of Human Rights in 2014.* Human Rights Commission of Pakistan, Lahore. http://hrcp-web.org/hrcpweb/data/HRCP%20Annual%20Report% 202014%20-%20English.pdf.

Hussain, K. (2012). *Rethinking education: Critical discourse and society.* Islamabad: Narratives.

Hussain, N. (2004). *Military rule, fundamentalism and the women's movement in Pakistan.* Lahore: ASR Publications.

Hussain, N., Mumtaz, S. and Choonara, S. (2005). *Politics of language.* Lahore: Simorgh Women's Resource and Publication Centre.

Hussain, N., Mumtaz, S. and Saigol, R. (Eds.) (1997). *Engendering the nation-state.* Lahore: Simorgh Women's Resource and Publication Centre.

48 *Lena Martinsson*

Khan, N. (Ed.) (2004). *Up against the state*. Lahore: ASR Publications.

Laclau, E. and Mouffe, C. (1985). *Hegemony and socialist strategy*. London and New York: Verso.

Mahmood, S. (2012). *Politics of piety*. Princeton, NJ: Princeton University Press.

Martinsson, L. (2016). Frictions and figurations: Gender equality norms meet activism. In L. Martinsson, G. Griffin and K.G. Nygren (Eds.), *Challenging the myth of gender equality in Sweden* (pp. 187–210). Bristol: Policy Press.

Martinsson, L. and Reimers, E. (Eds.) (2010). *Norm-struggles: Sexualities in contentions*. Newcastle upon Tyne: Cambridge Scholars Publishing.

Mian, Y. (2009). *CSR Pakistan*. Lahore: Capital Business Pakistan.

Mouffe, C. (1992). Feminist and radical politics. In J. Butler and J.W. Scott (Eds.), *Feminists theorize the political* (pp. 369–384). New York: Routledge.

Mouffe, C. (2005). *On the political*. Abingdon & New York: Routledge.

Mouffe, C. (2013). Hegemony and new political subjects. In J. Martin (Ed.), *Chantal Mouffe, Hegemony, radical democracy and the political* (pp. 45–57). London: Routledge.

Puhar, J.K. (2007). *Terrorist assemblage: Homonationalism in queer time*. Durham: Duke University Press.

Rofel, L. (2007). *Desiring China: Experiments in neoliberalism, sexuality, and public culture*. Durham: Duke University Press.

Shaikh, F. (2009). *Making sense of Pakistan*. London: Hurst & Company.

Siddiqui, S. (2012). *Education, inequalities, and freedom: A sociopolitical critique*. Islamabad: A Narratives Publication.

Siddiqui, S. (2014). *Language, gender and power: The politics of representation and hegemony in South Asia*. Karachi: Oxford University press.

Soomro, A. D., Khan, M. A., Kumar, M., Soomro, S. & Bohi, M. (2009). *The socio-economic conditions of carpet industry*. Jamshoro: University of Jamshoro.

Spivak, G.C. (1988). Can the subaltern speak? In C. Nelson and L. Grossberg (Eds.), *Marxism and the interpretation of culture* (pp. 271–313). London: Macmillan.

Spivak, G.C. (2008). *Other Asias*. Oxford: Blackwell Publishing.

Spivak, G.C. (2012). *An aesthetic education in the era of globalization*. London: Harvard University Press.

Sundhall, J. (2014). Betydelser av barns ålder I familjerättsliga utredningstexter. *Kvinder, Kön och Forskning* 1–2: 9–21.

Tsing, A.L. (2005). *Frictions: An ethnography of global connections*. Princeton, NJ: Princeton University Press.

4 Competition, accountability and performativity

Exploring schizoid neo-liberal 'equality objectives' in a UK primary school

Jos Harvey and Jessica Ringrose

Introduction

> We are building an Aspiration Nation, my dream for Britain is that opportunity is not an accident of birth, but a birthright . . . as Churchill said: 'we are for the ladder, let all try their best to climb'.
>
> (Prime Minister David Cameron 2013)

As noted throughout this book, the complex set of ideas that inform the concept of neo-liberalism are multifaceted and have been taken up widely to explain new processes of marketisation and new regimes of governance in schooling and education internationally. Davies and Bansel have effectively summarised this, speaking in the Australian context:

> The neoliberal management technologies that were installed included increased exposure to competition, increased accountability measures and the implementation of performance goals in the contracts of management.
>
> (Davies and Bansel 2007, p. 254)

Using these three themes – competition, accountability and performativity – we critically examine current UK Prime Minister David Cameron's notion that schools are somehow equalisers providing an 'equal opportunities' ladder for children to climb, regardless of their background. We explore how schools are now increasingly required to demonstrate that they are providing an equal service in terms of opportunity, access and experience, as set out in the Equalities Act (Great Britain Parliament 2010). We will argue that the pressure to prove an equalities outcome may actually eclipse everyday spaces and practises of social justice and equality in schools. Indeed, there are many who argue that what has been called a 'neo-liberal transformation' of the education system is contradictory, so whilst claiming to equalise opportunity, new aspects of performativity and competition, it introduces further deficit models and winner and loser models, in fact deepening inequalities in schools (Bradbury 2013; Carey 2014; Cross 2007; Gillborn 2010; Littler 2013; Lucey and Reay 2002).

50　*Jos Harvey and Jessica Ringrose*

Stephen Ball has been one of the most proficient critics of neo-liberal performativity and audit cultures in schools. He and his colleagues note accurately that England been one of the most advanced centres of neo-liberal policy experimentation and practise, forming a sort of laboratory for studying neo-liberalised policies, networks, enactments and effects in education (Ball 2003). Following this logic, in this chapter, we explore a case study of the implementation of so-called neo-liberal policy reforms in an East London primary school. We explore the development of the school's new equalities policy, a requirement under the Education Act 2010. Our main research objective was to question how so-called neo-liberal governmental policies were filtering into schools and impacting their equalities practises. Within this, we sought to broadly explore the following questions:

- How are policies and cultures affecting the ways in which staff members and school policymakers approach equalities?
- What are the contradictory or schizoid effects/affects of the new pressures?

To begin to think about these questions, we want to discuss in some greater detail three key aspects of neo-liberal policy formation as identified in the research literature: accountability, competition and performativity.

Accountability

In England, recent policy 'bias' towards academisation has led to some schools becoming increasingly distanced from local authority-led governance. This new neo-liberal autonomy (in contrast to the major state governance that emerged in the 1980s around the introduction of the National Curriculum) places a high degree of accountability on schools, as with greater freedom comes greater responsibility: 'Individual subjects have thus welcomed the increasing individualism as a sign of their freedom and, at the same time, institutions have increased competition, *responsibilisation* and the transfer of risk from the state to individuals at a heavy cost to many individuals' (Davies and Bansel 2007, p. 249). Responsibilisation of actors at various levels is key here, with schools being increasingly held to account using quantitative measures (Ball 2003; Bradbury 2013; Gillborn 2010), such as exam results, phonics screening tests and progress charts, measures often critiqued by those working in schools for being too narrow (Gillborn 2010; Martino and Rezai-Rashti 2013). As Yelland writes:

> Conservative forces have constructed and implemented an agenda that attempts to reduce educational outcomes to the minutiae of observable outcomes that can be demonstrated in simple tasks that require routine responses rather than consider the educational experience as engagement with people and ideas.
>
> (Yelland 2007, p. 9)

Ball argues that the increased levels of accountability have become 'terrors of performativity', which are internalised by educators (Ball 2003; Bradbury 2013) and normalised: 'a rationality that cannot imagine any other way to justify and evaluate preschools except in terms of their ability to produce pre-specified outcomes and through the application of measurement techniques that are assumed to be objective and universally valued' (Dahlberg and Moss 2004, p. 5). Here, Dahlberg and Moss are troubled by the over-reliance on specific outcomes to judge schools, suggesting that they may be unreliable and potentially too narrow to judge quality.

Competition

Neo-liberalism 'involves the alignment of public sector organisations with private sector values' (Bradbury 2013), and one of those values is competitiveness.

> In an internationally competitive marketplace, education plays a critical role in helping each nation to create and maintain a competitive edge . . . what has emerged is a new set of public policy demands for efficiency, accountability, effectiveness and flexibility, what Ball has described as a 'generic global policy ensemble'.
>
> (Maguire 2010, p. 41)

Maguire references the UK education system as a whole, competing with other nations through tests such as the Programme for International Student Assessment, but the competition filters through to individual schools. Bradbury (2013) references the 2011 Tickell review's guidelines: 'results should be published at national and local level so that the general public can hold government and local authorities to account for quality of Early Years services'. There are many competitive layers in schools: parents can state their preference for a school from a variety of competing local options, schools aspire to score a higher OFSTED grade in inspections and career reputations of senior leadership teams are at stake, enhanced by the introduction of performance-related pay (Ball 2003). (The Office for Standards in Education (OFSTED) is the testing and auditing system in the UK through which school performance is measured and disciplined.)

Some researchers argue that competition affects equalities because, as noted through Gillborn and Youdell's (1999) 'triage system' example, in a neo-liberal system, pupils are seen as 'commodities' to improve schools' outcomes. Using the metaphor of a medical crisis, Gillborn and Youdell use the idea of triage to show how limited resources are siphoned for the greatest benefit according to categories of predicted success and failure for students. Gillborn and Youdell applied this triage process to the educational context of streaming by math ability, showing the systematic process of directing educational resources to some pupils whilst neglecting others, the significant point being that fewer resources were directed towards students deemed 'hopeless cases', intensifying inequalities, particularly around 'race' in the UK (in Marks 2012: 58). Dudley-Marling and Baker (2012) describe, for example, how '[s]tudents with high test scores enhance the reputation and, hence, the marketability of charter schools. Students

52 *Jos Harvey and Jessica Ringrose*

who do not score well on tests threaten charters' competitiveness' (p. 141). One teacher participant in their study argued:

> Teachers don't want [difficult-to-educate students]. If my job depends on their test scores . . . I don't want those kids. I do because I am a teacher and went into teaching to help kids. But if my job depends on it . . . my car payments depend on it . . . my apartment payment depends on it . . . I don't want those kids.
>
> (Dudley-Marling and Baker 2012 p. 141)

The allusion to pupils as commodities was also used by one of Ball's interviewees, who felt that pupils were treated as 'mere nuts and bolts on a distant production line' (Ball 2003, p.221).

Performativity

Stephen Ball suggests that neo-liberalism has caused schools to focus on their outward 'performance', defining performativity as follows:

> Performativity is a technology, a culture and a mode of regulation that employs judgements, comparisons and displays as means of incentive, control, attrition and change based on rewards and sanctions (both material and symbolic). The performances (of individual subjects or organisations) serve as measures of productivity or output, or displays of 'quality', or 'moments' of promotion or inspection. As such they stand for, encapsulate or represent the worth, quality or value of an individual or organisation within a field of judgement.
>
> (Ball 2003, p. 217)

In this quotation, the link between performativity, accountability and competition is clear: performance is the mode in which schools present their accountability in the competitive field of education. Ball draws on Foucault to argue the importance of examining who controls the 'field of judgement', as he suggests that the decisions around what 'quality' or 'worthwhile' mean are inherently political. Ball argues that performativity has the potential to obscure moral judgements and lead establishment settings to introduce practises just because they look good to outsiders, even if they are believed to be a waste of time or even harmful: 'Not infrequently, the requirements of such systems bring into being unhelpful or indeed damaging practises, which nonetheless satisfy performance requirements' (Ball 2003, p. 220). Performativity affects the reasoning behind some educational practises: 'Are we doing this because it is important, because we believe in it, because it is worthwhile? Or is it being done ultimately because it will be measured or compared? It will make us look good!' (Ball 2003, p. 220). Ball's teacher participants in the study indicated a '*values schizophrenia*', in which they felt that performativity created a dualism between what they believe in and the pressure to perform in a certain way for outsiders. Ball (2003) argues: 'authenticity is replaced entirely by plasticity' (p. 15), by which he suggests that schools may adjust their malleable values to present the ethos that is attractive to those judging them.

In the next section, we will explore how these three aspects of accountability, competition and performativity play out in the research context under review, keeping this notion of values schizophrenia uppermost in our analysis.

The research case study

The primary methodology for our research was a qualitative case study of the creation of an equalities policy at a primary school in East London. The research involved several months of observing meetings with school policymakers, as well as observing pupil workshops in which they discussed equalities issues. The project was designed to explore the process by which the school created their new equalities policy. Previously, there were statutory requirements for schools to have disability and race equality policies, as well as to provide evidence of how the school supports children receiving free school meals (the government indicator for poverty). There were already statutory requirements around race, gender and disability, but schools are now asked to create a broader equalities policy that demonstrates how the school aims to promote equalities for all social groups. In our case study school, staff members, governors and the equalities officer from the borough were involved in creating the policy, and the school wanted to include 'pupil voice' in its creation as well. Overall, we hoped to observe and capture some of the processes involved in the creation of the equalities policy so that we could understand some of the thought processes behind how equalities are prioritised and how this intra-acts with the demands to 'perform' equality with contradictory, or what we explore as 'schizoid', effects that elide everyday experiences of inequality in primary school.

In the neo-liberalised 'audit culture', how have equalities issues become quantified?

Observations of school policymakers indicated a reliance on data, primarily test results, to identify inequalities that might exist in the setting. There are external pressures on schools which perhaps led to this school focusing on quantitative evidence to prove they are providing equality. For example, the Office for Standards in Education states the following:

> Equality is integral to the inspection framework and the promotion of equality of opportunity for all pupils underpins the school inspection framework. School inspection acts in the interests of children, young people and their parents. It encourages high-quality provision that meets diverse needs and promotes not just equality of opportunity but improving outcomes for all pupils regardless of background.
>
> (OFSTED 2014, p. 4)

This quotation from OFSTED clearly states that schools are required to provide not just opportunities but **outcomes**, the most obvious and measurable outcomes being equal test results amongst different groups. The focus on test results is not new: educational trajectories have long focused on pupils' major exam results or qualifications from O-Levels to GCSEs; however, inspections now place responsibility on the school to a) achieve certain percentages in tests or be deemed 'failing' and b) ensure that all social groups perform equally. Schools are therefore under pressure to demonstrate to OFSTED that their school is meritocratic: that everyone can and does achieve 'regardless of background'. It is perhaps worth noting here that, whilst OFSTED previously monitored progress through a 'contextual value added' score, inspection is now purely focused on outcome and achievement.

In our case study, the school policymakers immediately used data from test results to identify inequalities. They used a variety of data, primarily through the site RAISEonline, which separates children's test results into different social groups, for example, according to race. An example of a table used by the school policymakers can be seen below.

Key stage 2 exam results 2014

In observing the school policymakers, it could be seen how, at a first superficial level, they deduced the following perception from the data:

> *Boys and girls achieve the same SATs results. Generally, every year, there's no gap in results, so gender is not an issue here.*

Here, the use of test results suggests a narrowing of gender issues to specific, measurable outcomes of exam achievement, but as Martino and Rezai-Rashti (2013) argue, 'numbers, as inscription devices are not able to capture the messy, hybrid realities of people's lives today and can elide the complexity of schools in their various contexts' (p. 295). This example could be described as a 'microcosm' for the national attitude to gender gap discourse and a moral panic over girls outperforming boys in exams such as the GCSEs, evidenced by news articles with headlines such as, 'Boys lagging behind girls' (Burns 2014) and 'Are boys catching up with girls?' (Telegraph 2012), as well as policy initiatives such as 'Supporting Boys with Writing' (DfE 2008, see Ringrose 2013). Analysing the statement 'gender is not an issue here' through a feminist lens, one could argue that using test results alone 'rips gender out of a sociocultural context' and creates a context of invisibility and silence around a range of issues related to gender, sexuality and well-being at school (Ringrose 2007, p. 473).

An intersectional feminist approach (Gillborn and Mirza 2000; Showunmi 2011) questions the limitations of the data that can be used to present the simplified idea that girls are 'doing fine' and enjoying 'success' (Ringrose 2007). For instance, Victoria Showunmi (2011) uses qualitative approaches to challenge the quantitative 'evidence' that suggests all girls are succeeding at school. Showunmi's interviews with black female pupils showed that although black girls were academically successful, suggesting that their race and gender were no barriers to achievement; in reality, their background had a wide impact on their experiences

Table. 4.1 Anonymous Primary School Key Stage 2 Test Results

	Disadvantaged pupils*	Other pupils
Percentage of disadvantaged pupils achieving level 3 or below in reading and math tests and writing TA	9%	6%
Percentage of disadvantaged pupils achieving level 4 or above in reading and math tests and writing TA	74%	88%
Percentage of disadvantaged pupils achieving level 4B or above in reading and math tests and writing TA	53%	71%
Percentage of disadvantaged pupils achieving level 5 or above in reading and math tests and writing TA	19%	35%
Percentage of disadvantaged pupils making at least 2 levels of progress in reading	86%	94%
Percentage of disadvantaged pupils making at least 2 levels of progress in writing TA	88%	94%
Percentage of disadvantaged pupils making at least 2 levels of progress in math	91%	94%

of equality in school. Showunmi's participants demonstrated that ethnicity/gender impacted their aspirations, the ways they were stereotyped and the expectations people had of them: 'loud and destructive', 'there is no individuality when you are black, you are black, she's black, we are all black' (Showunmi 2011, p. 8).

Whereas gender is treated as a non-issue, the statistical 'gap' in achievement between pupils receiving free school meals (indicator for poverty) and those from more affluent backgrounds was treated with utmost concern by school policy-makers, who felt compelled to come up with an explanation and response to the presentation of inequality, as evident through observations of meetings:

> *Meeting One: The head teacher seemed particularly worried about justifying why children from poorer backgrounds achieved lower results. She spoke about the need to explain why, saying: 'I could tell you exactly why each of these children achieved low results'.*
>
> *Meeting One: Staff seem particularly frustrated because they can 'tell the stories' of each pupil who is underachieving . . . but the test results suggest they are failing.*

The policymakers' responses to the data indicate several things. Firstly, they suggest that the school policymakers involved feel that the data is insufficient: it presents the idea that the school is failing pupils, when in fact, the staff know there are other reasons which contribute to those pupils' underachievement. This is symptomatic of the 'schizoid' context we are exploring, where the numbers suggest a simple gap and solution which discount the knowledge of staff and pupils. Martino and Rezai-Rashti (2013) write about how this process operates in wide-scale international testing and ranking procedures such as the Programme for International Student Assessment: 'PISA acknowledges that there are other influences to socioeconomic disadvantage, such as family circumstances, mental health and housing, but they fail to include them, so accountability lies purely with the school' (p. 598).

Secondly, the comments suggest that the school policymakers are going to focus on the 'rich-poor' pupil gap, even though they view the data as misleading, because they are required to 'justify' the data. Due to the pressure to demonstrate income equality, this issue has thus become prioritised. Using Ball's analyses of performativity and fabrications, one could argue that this situation is an example of performativity under pressure: the data presented becomes the focus. Ball writes: 'Authenticity is replaced by plasticity. Within the education market institutional promotion and representation take on the qualities of postmodern depthlessness – yet more floating signifiers in the plethora of semiotic images, spectacles and fragments that increasingly dominate consumer society' (Ball 2000, p. 15). In this context, 'authenticity' could refer to the children's experiences of inequality, and the data – such as exam results, often presented as colour-coded, numerated boxes on a spreadsheet – could be the 'plethora of semiotic images'. However, these signifiers are also limited in that they reduce all meaning to the measurement referent, which is key in audit and performativity market driven cultures.

Thirdly, through the policymakers' desire to 'tell the stories' of the children at the same time as they feel compelled to respond to the measurement results, they actually reject the quantitative data as a useful tool. They suggest that quantitative data is unable to present the complex life of a child and the reasons behind their (under)achievement. However, Gillborn argues:

> A growing trend in education policy and classroom practise is to assume a blinkered perspective that focuses on each individual case and denies the relevance of the wider picture. In the face of failing statistics, we see a swing to the micro. This approach sounds fair enough – judge every question on its individual merits – but what this really achieves is a denial of inequality . . . It is only when we stand back from the detail of the individual case (and see that certain groups are hugely over-represented in exclusions, in lower sets, and in the ranks of the under-achieving) that the racist nature of the processes becomes clear.
>
> (Gillborn 2001, p. 109)

Gillborn advocates the use of statistics here, and arguably, our observations support his view that quantitative data around social groups can prevent schools from denying inequality. But, again, we find this relates back strongly to the idea of 'schizophrenic values' having to be juggled by staff members, contradictions that can put staff in an impossible situation, caught between large-scale numbers about achievement and individualism. Since the government uses statistics around performance only in ways that suit them and sets up achievement 'gaps' rather than showing evidence of systematic sexism or racism in institutions, individuals can be called to blame in relation to achievement gaps. Neo-liberal-informed achievement policies are actually used to attribute success or failure to the individual (Lucey and Reay 2002).

Taking race as an example, in the relatively recent 2011 riots that engulfed the UK, the prime minister argued:

> Let's be clear. These riots were not about race . . . These riots were not about government cuts . . . And these riots were not about poverty . . . No, this was about behaviour. People showing indifference to right and wrong. People with a twisted moral code. People with a complete absence of self-restraint.
> (Prime Minister David Cameron: 2011)

Here, the prime minister, in blaming individuals' behaviour, essentially removes all sociological factors, such as the connection between welfare, poverty and rioting, and removes all responsibility from the state, such as the suggestion that cuts in services for poorer communities or historic problems around policing and the black community could be responsible for the riots. The message is obvious: this is not the state's fault; this is the individuals' fault.

This approach is also now being used by schools, especially academies (Wilkins 2012). Schools can argue that the reason some pupils fail is because they are lazy, unmotivated or poorly behaved, for example, and exclusion is increasingly used in secondary school as a means to oust problematic students (Youdell 2012).

As we found in our observations in primary schools, the neo-liberal accountability pressures on achievement in schools creates a contradictory situation: if a pupil fails, the school owns that failure and is potentially sanctioned for it, and no excuses can be made about the individual. The school is under greater pressure to help pupils succeed, while presumably this should prevent groups, such as black boys who persistently underachieve, being blamed for their failure on an individual basis. However, research indicates that this is not actually what is happening; other policies, such as behavioural policies, can be used to sanction, exclude and further marginalise those groups deemed 'vulnerable' through the statistical achievement data (Youdell 2012).

What happens in a primary school environment when race and gender equalities are reduced to audit culture measurements?

In the previous section, we noted that school policymakers focused on data such as test results to identify inequalities. However, through the policy formation process, the school also sought to gain children's insights into equalities issues at the school. Here, we analyse the pupils' views on equality in the setting and compare these to the equalities issues deduced from quantitative data. The first question pupils were asked was, 'What is equality?'

Navid: When everyone's equal.
Satnam: No separate places for black and white people.

58   *Jos Harvey and Jessica Ringrose*

Arafath: No one's treated badly, we're all treated the same way.
Navid: Everyone has the same rights, everybody's the same.

When asked how the school promotes equality, the pupils said:

Rizwan: In the playground, there everyone's treated fairly, like you wouldn't make fun of people with disabilities.
Satnam: You might include new children. Everyone should participate.
Navid: You wouldn't tease people about low levels.
Rizwan: Staff might take advantage of disabled children. I'm not saying it happens here, but they might give someone smaller portions if they're disabled because they can't stand up for themselves.
Tanisha: No limits to books, everyone of all ages can borrow whatever they want.
Rizwan: Everyone gets the same amount of food; they have equal play time.
Navid: We're allowed to have democratic votes on things, like voting on what rewards we want.

Some of these quotations link well to the Equalities Act's 'protected characteristics', such as ethnicity, which are monitored quantitatively through test results. Importantly, though, the children's thoughts go beyond the protected characteristics, including 'axes of difference', such as 'being new' or 'having low levels', so they bring new aspects to the policy discourse here. Whilst the adults focus on the characteristics measured by the government, the children bring in those and more, suggesting that they have a more intersectional perspective than the adults or perhaps that their reality evidences a complexity of equalities that go beyond governance expectations and beyond what can be quantified.

Whilst 'gap discourse' dictates that school policymakers must focus on gaps in statistics, a fairly abstract notion for children, the pupils have a wider, more holistic attitude to equalities and well-being. The pupils' examples are rooted in their everyday reality: issues that occur in the playground and the school lunch queue, which offer more practical examples of equalities as lived experience. We want to introduce several further examples of how students' experiences related to equalities issues refute the comparative statistically driven logics of performativity audit culture.

Gender

The following conversation was observed in a workshop with School Council members.

Session 3:

The children saw some other, very young, boys and girls playing together in the playground.

Satnam: Wow, that's nice they're playing together. It's easier for young kids [boys and girls] to play together because they don't know the consequences.

Teacher:	What are the consequences?
Navid:	Because sometimes you get picked on for being friends with girls.
Satnam:	It's partly because the other kids think you might fancy them.
Navid:	Other kids think we might do bad things.
Teacher:	What do you mean by bad things?
Satnam:	They figure out about . . . you say it Navid!
Navid:	Um, kissing.
Satnam:	Yeah, but worse, you know, S-E-X. If you're friends with a boy, they spread rumours that you're doing it even when they're false.
Teacher:	So are you saying that when children realise that boys and girls can have sex, they start teasing each other for being friends with boys or girls?
Navid/Satnam:	Yeah.
Teacher:	So when would you stop being friends with boys or girls?
Satnam:	Um, probably about Y3.
Navid:	But you know what, it's good for boys and girls to be friends with each other; it's good to be used to it for when you're older, for when you have to get married.
Teacher:	But do you have to get married?
Both:	In our culture yes; in our religion you have to, so it's good to get used to it.

This conversation between two pupils illuminates gender complexities and nuances that are totally bypassed in the achievement gap discourses. Firstly, the pupils show awareness of sexuality which impacts on the social cohesion of boys and girls as friendships become 'romanticised' (Kehler 2007; Renold 2003). Renold writes: 'simple mixed-sex interactions like borrowing a pencil or helping with a class-task could be (hetero)sexualised (usually by teasing the boy/girl involved that they "fancy" each other)' (Renold 2003, p. 190). This is an example of how qualitative data has identified an equalities issue that cannot be drawn from the quantitative test results that the school policymakers used. Nonetheless, gendered power relations and sexuality are clearly issues identified strongly by the children. Furthermore, this conversation suggests that equalities issues need to be contextualised and are intersectional. The pupils involved within this conversation are Muslim, as are 90% of the pupils in the school. Within this context, comments such as 'in our religion you have to [get married]' and 'get used to it' need to be viewed intersectionally to observe how religion, gender and sexuality intersect to produce equalities issues (Youdell 2012). For example, one could argue that these comments suggest heteronormative attitudes or issues around arranged marriages in the community.

Race/Religion

'Ethnicity' is often presented as a 'variable' in data such as exam results, although statistics are often discredited (Bradbury 2013; Cross 2007; Gillborn 2010) as assessments are seen as far from neutral. The pupils' views on race and ethnicity were far too complex to be presented as a point on a graph.

Tia: If there's someone on their own, whatever their religion, you ask them to play with you.
Teacher: How would you know their religion?
Tia: Their skin.
Tara: If you're friends with someone from another religion, you might get bullied by others; they say bad things are going to happen to you.

This small conversation suggests that pupils have conflated religion with skin colour, highlighting a lack of awareness about race and religion, but furthermore, it suggests that religious prejudice might exist within the school. Again, this is context specific and intersectional. The OFSTED guidance on equality prioritises outcomes, but these quotations bring that into question. Firstly, it ignores equality of experience for all religious groups. Secondly, the outcomes measured are test-achievement focused, and they fail to measure whether the pupils have the religious tolerance to work cohesively in our diverse, multicultural society, which would appear to be essential in a climate where schools are expected to monitor extremism and promote 'British values'.

Meritocracy

Though the pupils would most probably be unaware of the quantitative measures used to identify the income-based inequalities in their school, they seemed to subvert the idea of meritocracy in our observations. Considering the huge focus on levels both nationwide and within this school, it is noteworthy that the pupils referred to them just twice.

Peter: You wouldn't tease people about low levels.
Tia: Children who are good at sports get picked more.
Rebecca: Yeah, that's unfair.
Tia: If you are good at football, you get to be on the school team, so you can play after school, go to matches . . .
Peter: If you have low levels, people won't want you to be in their group.
Katie: Yeah, you might be picked last for groups.

Schools, and the school inspectors, focus on improving achievement: aiming for higher percentages of pupils to reach certain levels. Nowhere in our observations, and rarely in policy, do adults refer to equality for lower achievers, but the children here mention this group several times. The children show a protective attitude, suggesting that you 'wouldn't tease people about low levels', and they show concern for the social impact of 'low levels', but they never refer to the need to raise pupils' levels, in contrast to the policymakers' attitude. The pupils also express resentment of 'elitism' within football: they are advocating equal opportunities for everyone, regardless of ability.

Competition 61

To summarise, the pupils' insights suggest that the equality issues they experience go far beyond the issues that can be interpreted through data on exam results: they cannot be presented quantitatively. Firstly, some of the equality issues raised, such as 'being new', are not measured, and therefore they are absent from the data adults use to identify inequalities. Secondly, whilst the test results for boys and girls were equal, this does not mean that there are no gender issues in the school. The gender issues were complex and irreducible to a table or statistics: there were issues with equality of experience. Thirdly, the test results measure equality of outcome in a very narrow, purely academic, way: they fail to indicate whether the pupils have the skills to be cohesive citizens, for example, whether they are tolerant of religions and ethnicities. Finally, the government, OFSTED and schools present equalities as the ability of all groups to reach top levels, whereas the children wanted everyone to be treated equally regardless of their level, which is perhaps an ideological clash between the pupils and the policymakers.

In a 'neo-liberalised' society, perhaps the prioritisation of equalities issues by various actors equates to their currency in the actors' world. Governmental policymakers arguably focus on school outcomes, such as test results, because they know that in our neo-liberal society, qualifications hold currency in the job market, whereas even a great deal of progress in school won't really be credible if the achievement isn't good enough. In this line of thought, it could be argued that the pupils are not 'forward-looking' in their identification of equalities issues, because what matters and what holds currency in their world at age 10 is different to what matters in the adult world. However, I would argue that this discredits some very valuable insights they give, because certainly many of the equalities issues they raise have broad implications for the future. For example, in the borough where the school is situated there is high unemployment, particularly for women, and the issues around marriage being obligatory in 'our culture', the lack of cohesion between boys and girls and the inherited prejudice around socialising with different religious groups have huge potential implications not only for pupils' social futures and how we are progressing as a society but, in economic terms, their employability, too.

Equality outcomes

Towards the final stages of our equality case study, we turned to the outcomes of the policy formation. As noted previously in the chapter, outcomes are of high value in the neo-liberal school because they are pivotal to performativity and accountability. One of the outputs of the equality policy-formation process was the creation and distribution of posters around the school. The local education authority designed and printed hundreds of copies of these posters on glossy paper, aimed at informing pupils about the new equality policy. What makes this poster particularly relevant is that it is a very typical example of the types of display schools use to communicate equal opportunities.

The main feature of the poster is a group of bright, smiling cartoon animals: a zebra, a tiger, a hippo – all various sizes and diverse shapes and colours, but all

62   Jos Harvey and Jessica Ringrose

happily grouped together. Multicoloured handprints, pink, red, green, border the page with writing in bold: 'We believe in creating a school community where everyone can reach their potential, regardless of background'.

There are several ways to use the critiques of neo-liberalism we have been developing in the chapter to analyse this poster. Firstly, the image on the poster shows a variety of cartoon animals of different species, shapes and sizes. Though we cannot be sure what the intention behind this image was, it is reasonable to suggest that it adopts the 'no matter what we look like, we are all the same' equalities trope. Following this argument, this image could be viewed as a 'fabrication' (Ball 2003), because, as Ball argues, whether true or not the purpose of the poster is to signify equality. It is a quick visual representation of the ethos the institution needs to present. We see an over-arching message that colour/shape/size/gender/species mean nothing, and no matter what we look like, we are all the same – but these are neo-liberal messages! Images like these invoke a discourse of meritocracy, that we are all equal. But they are devoid of context and meaning – they are what Stuart Hall might call an empty or floating signifier. Animals are notorious for filling this function in children's storybooks, to de-racialise (a purple elephant) and de-sexualise (gender and sexually neutral, one of each species) subjectivity (Chetty 2014). Some of the effects of this use of animals are to deny or mystify the ability to think about social complexity in relation to structural inequalities according to race, class and gender.

By viewing this image through a Critical Race Theory (CRT) lens, we can consider how the poster is purposefully 'colour blind'. In this case, endemic racialised power differentials in British society are *purposefully* obscured through the use of the brightly coloured animals rather than realistically coloured human children attending the school. CRT investigates institutionalised racism, including the tactics of white supremacy, privilege and power in UK society (Gillborn 2014. Through this lens of CRT we see that the poster: 1) wilfully obscures attention to racism or racial power differentials in society (colour blind) and 2) suggests that just because people are different, that does not mean they are not also somehow equal (meritocracy). Gillborn (2014, p. 2) notes in relation to wilfully denying racism in educational processes that 'neo-liberalism typically works through colour-blind language that dismisses the saliency of race-specific analyses'.

These logics, as we have suggested above, are again schizoid and confusing, as they fly in the face of staff's and children's own lived experiences, which are infused with ideas of race and power. For example, in the workshops, pupils had conversations such as the following:

Staff member: How would you know their religion?
Pupil: Their skin.

But these nuances and confusions about how race and skin are read by the children are not addressed through the metaphor of multicoloured animals. As Chetty (2014) argues about popular picture books that tackle 'race' issues:

> The story's irony is that it removes difference at the very point that it highlights it – that is to say, it removes a particular kind of difference (social

inequality) whilst highlighting another (superficial bodily markers), which, once decontextualised, is rendered socially insignificant. And so a book about difference becomes in fact a book about sameness, consistent with 'colour-blindness'.

(p. 20)

Even more ironic is the fact that animals are not the same. They each have their position in the food chain, and some are more powerful, faster and stronger than others, which perhaps contradicts the idea that pupils are all the same and their successes can be based around the same exams. As the now-famous aphorism suggests:

Everybody is a genius, but if you judge a fish by its ability to climb a tree it will live its whole life believing it is stupid.

(Albert Einstein)

Thinking about issues of gender and sexuality, arguably some of the points in the poster do relate to pupils' comments about fairness for boys and girls, but these are abstracted to the point of obscurity – no one would dispute them, but what do they mean? Indeed, the aims are very closely linked to the language of the Equalities Act 2010, which leaves us wondering if there would be space on this poster for actually addressing the messy, sticky issues that pupils raised, such as the romanticisation of boy/girl friendships or territorialising space according to gendered bodies and sport (football). Kelley writes that when we involve children in the policymaking process, 'typically, we are seeking a response to or endorsement of an idea that already exists' (Kelley 2006, p. 37). Perhaps a neo-liberal effect on pupil voice is that the pressure on schools to perform and be accountable is so intense that it leaves no space for ideas that hold content about particular issues, such as childhood sexuality, which are deemed too risky to engage with (Renold et al. 2015). So what we find is a schizoid contradiction (Renold and Ringrose 2011), an artefact that symbolically performs an equality objective at the same time as it obscures its actual referent, which is to promote equality amongst children who, because of differential relationships to axiomatic structures/discourses and relations power, are not equally positioned to climb up Churchill and Cameron's social ladder. Significantly, negotiating these highly contradictory policies and practises is also felt keenly as a schizoid pressure to perform equalities in ways that do not address the lived relations of inequalities among staff and teachers and students attempting to work in these contexts.

Conclusion

Throughout this chapter, research from our case study school in East London gave rich, qualitative insight into the ways neo-liberal discourses impact (infect, interrupt) equality practises in schools. We can deduce from this research that some of the key impacts of neo-liberal trends are increased competition, accountability and performativity that force, at least this school, to focus on quantitative results as the key indicator for inequalities. Furthermore, our research found

64   *Jos Harvey and Jessica Ringrose*

that the subsequent effects of over-reliance on quantitative data in neo-liberal equalities practises are multiple and contradictory. Some of the effects included the pressure to 'perform' equality, which staff experienced in a schizoid way, since they were meant to focus on issues such as a 'rich-poor' pupil 'gap' but discount their own knowledge of the complexity of class-based and economic social inequality. Regarding gender, as has been evident in years of 'failing boys' panics in the UK (Epstein et al. 1998), the quantitative statistics in this school that rendered gender a non-issue did not match pupils' comments on the issues that affected them, shoring up contradictions between the statistical evidence and lived experience. Rather, we illustrated that pupils noted a multitude of gender- and sexuality-related issues affecting them that the focus on exam results between girls and boys wilfully ignores (Ringrose 2013). Likewise, we illustrated how racial power and difference were made invisible in the equality policy poster, using Critical Race Theory to raise questions about institutionalised racism.

Our research indicates that the neo-liberal focus on outcomes potentially leads schools to over-invest in 'fabrications' that signify equality but fail to grapple with issues affecting children. Overall, our research raises questions about neo-liberal pressure to identify equalities issues quantitatively and points to the need for a strongly intersectional approach that considers the complex play of indicators around race, religion, social class, gender and sexuality and ability in thinking through issues of attainment.

Turning to recommendations of our research, we feel it is important to conclude by mentioning some of the potentially positive aspects of the policy-making engagement process that are of course not reducible or able to be captured in the poster we examined. As Maguire et al. (2011) have noted, policy enactment is a messy process, and many issues were brought to light and grappled with in a productive way. For instance, as referenced throughout the chapter, the pupils' comments widely alluded to a number of gender issues within the school: the boys' awareness of 'oppressive masculinity' and the prohibition of male emotion, the segregation of boys and girls in the playground, the sexualisation of boy/girl friendships, the stereotyping of girls and the heteronormativity of the schooling. Once the policymakers were made aware of the pupils' views, they took them seriously. School policymakers have presented several assemblies about gender, and they refused to relegate gender to a non-issue, as had happened at the beginning of the process, where the statistical comparisons between gender results on exams was the only measure of equality. Policymakers actually listened to the pupils' comments on gender and noted that they were important and needed addressing. Promoting gender equality around sports, for instance, was written into the policy, taking into account pupils' idea that sports could promote gender equality. The school heavily promoted the women's World Cup, assigning each class a team to promote women's sport, and they took the girls' football team to a women's event at a stadium. This suggests a very high level of investment of time and energy from the school and of participation from pupils, showing the desire to address equality. The powerful impact pupils' insights into equalities had on this school's practise (and the school's willingness to listen to those pupils) can be seen as a strong example of the potential that exists to address equalities beyond simplistically showing evidence of lessening 'gaps' in quantitative data.

And yet, the remnants of the policy push to compare and equalise around a binary formation of gender comparisons, for instance, remained. One staff member expressed concern, saying: *'We've gone gender mad, but I think we've done too much about "girl power"; we need to talk about how boys are affected by male stereotypes too'*. In our view, this statement is useful to conclude with because it powerfully underscores the need for further equalities work that can keep challenging the boys vs. girls mentality (and the range of other 'gap talk' showcased by Gillborn and others) that comes out of statistical comparisons of achievement by group. The statement demonstrates, then, just how important it remains for policymakers to look beyond neo-liberal-fuelled data and tick-box outcomes to think about pupils' experiences and teachers' views in order to truly grapple with inequality as power differentials organised around intersecting aspects of race, class and gender, differentials and power relations that are not reducible to comparative points on an 'equalities objectives' graph.

References

Ball, S.J. (2000). Performativities and fabrications in the education economy: Towards the performative society? *The Australian Educational Researcher* 27(2): 1–23.

Ball, S.J. (2003). The teacher's soul and the terrors of performativity. *Journal of Education Policy* 18(2): 215–228.

Bradbury, A. (2013). *Understanding early years inequality: Policy, assessment and young children's identities.* London: Routledge.

Burns J. (2014). *Boys of 5 Lagging Behind Girls in Literacy and Numeracy,* Accessed online, 7 June 2016. Available at: http://www.bbc.co.uk/news/education-29651924.

Cameron, D. (2011). *PM's Speech on the Fightback after the Riots.* Prime Minister's Office. Online. Available at: https://www.gov.uk/government/speeches/pms-speech-on-the-fightback-after-the-riots

Cameron, D. (Rt Hon MP) *Speech to the National Conservative Convention.* Conservative Party Spring Forum, 16 March 2013.

Carey, R.L. (2014). A cultural analysis of the achievement gap discourse challenging the language and labels used in the work of school reform. *Urban Education* 49(4): 440–468.

Chetty, D. (2014). The elephant in the room: Picture books, philosophy for children and racism. *Childhood & Philosophy* 10(19): 11–31.

Cross, B.E. (2007). Urban school achievement gap as a metaphor to conceal US apartheid education. *Theory into Practice* 46(3): 247–255.

Dahlberg, G. and Moss, P. (2004). *Ethics and politics in early childhood education.* London: Routledge.

Davies, B. and Bansel, P. (2007). Neoliberalism and education. *International Journal of Qualitative Studies in Education* 20(3): 247–259.

Department for Education (2008) Gateway to Writing – Boys and writing. *The National Strategies,* Accessed online 7 June 2016. Available at http://www.foundationyears.org.uk/wp-content/uploads/2011/11/Gateway-to-Writing-Boys-and-writing.pdf

Dudley-Marling, C. and Baker, D. (2012). The effects of market-based school reforms on students with disabilities. *Disability Studies Quarterly* 32(2).

Epstein, D., Elwood, J., Hey, V. and Maw, J. (1998). *Failing boys? Issues in gender and achievement.* Buckingham, UK: Open University Press.

66 *Jos Harvey and Jessica Ringrose*

Gillborn, D. (2001). 'Raising standards' or rationing education? Racism and social justice in policy and practice. *Support for Learning, 16*(3), 105–111.

Gillborn, D. (2010). The colour of numbers: Surveys, statistics and deficit-thinking about race and class. *Journal of Education Policy* 25(2): 253–276.

Gillborn, D. (2014). Racism as policy: A critical race analysis of education reforms in the United States and England. *The Educational Forum* 78(1): 26–41.

Gillborn, D. and Mirza, H.S. (2000). Mapping race, class and gender: A synthesis of research evidence. London: Office for Standards in Education.

Gillborn, D. and Youdell, D. (1999). *Rationing education: Policy, practice, reform, and equity*. Buckingham, UK: Open University Press.

Great Britain Parliament (2010). *Equality Act 2010*: Elizabeth II. Available at: http://www.legislation.gov.uk/ukpga/2010/15/contents.

Kehler, M.D. (2007). Hallway fears and high school friendships: The complications of young men (re)negotiating heterosexualized identities. *Discourse: Studies in the Cultural Politics of Education* 28(2): 259–277.

Kelley, N. (2006). Children's involvement in policy formation. *Children's Geographies* 4(1): 37–44.

Littler, J. (2013). Meritocracy as plutocracy: The marketing of 'equality' under neo-liberalism. *New Formations: A Journal of Culture/Theory/Politics* 80(80): 52–72.

Lucey, H. and Reay, D. (2002). Carrying the beacon of excellence: social class differentiation and anxiety at a time of transition. *Journal of Education Policy, 17*(3), 321–336.

Maguire, M. (2010). Towards a sociology of the global teacher. In M. Apple, S. Ball and L. Gandin (Eds.), *The Routledge international handbook of the sociology of education* (pp. 58–68). London: Routledge.

Maguire, M., Ball, S. and Braun, A. (2011). *How schools do policy: Policy enactments in secondary schools*. London: Routledge.

Marks, R. (2012). "I get the feeling that it is really unfair": Educational triage in primary mathematics. *Proceedings of the British Society for Research into Learning Mathematics, 32*(2), 58–63.

Martino, W. and Rezai-Rashti, G. (2013). 'Gap talk' and the global rescaling of educational accountability in Canada. *Journal of Education Policy* 28(5): 589–611.

OFSTED (2014). *Inspecting equalities*. Accessed online, 2 August 2015. Available at: www.ofsted.gov.uk/resources/091097/

Paton, G. (2012). A-level results 2012: boys claim more A* grades than girls. *The Telegraph: 16th August 2012.*

Renold, E. (2003). 'If you don't kiss me, you're dumped': Boys, boyfriends and heterosexualised masculinities in the primary school. *Educational Review* 55(2): 179–194.

Renold, E., Egan, D. and Ringrose, J. (2015). Introduction. *Children, sexuality and sexualisation*. London: Palgrave.

Renold, E. and Ringrose, J. (2011). Schizoid subjectivities? Re-theorising teen-girls' sexual cultures in an era of 'sexualisation'. *Journal of Sociology* 47(4): 389–409.

Ringrose, J. (2007). Successful girls? Complicating post-feminist, neoliberal discourses of educational achievement and gender equality. *Gender and Education* 19(4): 471–489.

Ringrose, J. (2013). *Postfeminist education? Girls and the sexual politics of schooling*. London: Routledge.

Showunmi, V. (2011). *The research forum for the child*. Institute of Education, University of London.

Wilkins, A. (2012). Public battles and private takeovers: Academies and the politics of educational governance. *Journal of Pedagogy* 3(1): 11–29.

Yelland, N. (2007). Series editor's introduction. In J.A. Hatch (Ed.), *Early childhood qualitative research*. New York, London: Routledge, ix.

Youdell, D. (2012). Fabricating 'Pacific Islander': Pedagogies of expropriation, return and resistance and other lessons from a 'Multicultural Day'. *Race Ethnicity and Education* 15(2), 141–155.

5 Towards de-cold-war politics
Nationalism, democracy and new politics of/for education in Japan

Keita Takayama

De-cold-war politics in Asia

Almost 30 years have passed since the 'end' of cold-war geopolitics, marked by the demise of communism, the breakup of the Soviet Union and the removal of the Berlin Wall. There was much celebration of the global spread of capitalist economy and the universalisation of liberal democracy as bringing progress all around the world. The declaration of 'the end of history' – or the inevitable 'triumph' of liberal capitalist democracy – served to justify the dominating role that the United States (US) played in world political affairs thereafter. In this so-called 'post-political' world, it was believed that the antagonism between the Left and Right in the domestic political scene would soon disappear, and ideological conflicts would be replaced by consensual or dialogic liberal politics (cf. Mouffe 2005).

And yet, the spell of cold-war politics continues to shape politics and subjectivities in Asia (Chen 2010). Indeed, the United States' cold-war geopolitical interests have powerfully conditioned post-war politics in Asia, particularly in East Asia. The rise of developmentalist state regimes in Korea, Japan, Taiwan and Singapore was underpinned by the US's strategic interests in keeping socialist influence at bay in the region. These countries, often ruled by pro-capitalist, military and undemocratically 'elected' leaders, received considerable economic and military 'support' from the US, which contributed to their rapid economic growth throughout the 1960s and 1970s (Chen 2010). Moving into the post-political world, many of these countries are gradually transitioning out of the cold-war political configuration, and yet, its legacies are not completely behind them yet. Many visible reminders remain in the region, including the South–North divide of the Korean peninsula; the disproportionate concentration of US military bases in Okinawa, the southernmost island of Japan; and the economic and political dependency of Japan, Korea and Taiwan on the US.

The dependency of these East Asian countries on the US extends beyond economy and politics. Kuan Hsing Chen (2010) claims that 'the Cold War is still alive within us (Asians)' (p. 118), pointing to the overwhelming presence of the US in popular culture and people's habits, ideas, languages and even their desires and aspirations and hence their subjectivities. In order to release subjectivities in the region from the dead hand of the Cold War, therefore, he suggests that those in Asia need to engage in 'de-cold-war' politics, that is, to 'confront the legacies and continuing tensions of the Cold War' so as to 'reopen the past for reflection in order to make moments of liberation possible in the future' (p. x). To put it in my own words, Chen suggests that those in Asia must first of all understand the roles that the US has played in the historical formation of their geopolitical context and structure of knowledge and sentiment and then learn to enact what he calls, after Yoshimi Takeuchi, 'Asia as method', a strategy to shift the point of reference from the US to Asia so that new political subjectivities can emerge.

Taking cues from Chen's call for 'de-cold-war' politics in Asia, this chapter examines how the debate over nationalism (e.g., 'love of country') in Japanese education has been conditioned by the same cold-war legacy. More specifically, I will begin by analysing how the cold-war geopolitical context in the region has shaped the historical formation of post-war politics of education in Japan. Then I will demonstrate how this cold-war legacy continues to constrain the ongoing debate over nationalism in education, more specifically, the discussion about the role of schools for the development of national sentiment in Japan. For this I will review the existing scholarly critiques of nationalism in schools among some of the most prominent Japanese education scholars. The review will illuminate how their categorical rejection of nationalism has rendered invisible its constitutive roles for democratic polity and redistributive justice, while preventing a careful consideration of the possible roles that schools can play in channelling nationalistic passions into forces that are conducive to democratic polity. Finally, I will explore the possibility of a new politics of nationalism that extends beyond the cold-war spell, aiming for the redefinition of what counts as politics in education and by extension the reconstitution of political and national subjectivities through Japanese schooling. I will situate these analyses and explorations in the larger socio-political context of neoliberalism, where nationalism has come to assume renewed political meanings and functions.

The cold-war spell

The historical formation of Japanese politics of education is inseparably tied to the US cold-war hegemony in Asia. It was through the US Occupation (1945–1952) in the immediate aftermath of the Second World War that the US became deeply embedded in the structure of post-war Japanese politics. The occupation initially focused on demolishing, through extensive demilitarisation and democratisation programs, the totalitarian imperial regime which led the destructive war. However, the US government was also wary of the growing spread of socialism in Japan at the time. As a result, instead of completely destroying the Japanese imperial system that had played a crucial role in driving Japan into the destructive war, the US sought to reconstitute the symbolic authority of Emperor Hirohito to maintain Japan as a crucial anti-communist ally in Asia (Johnson 2004; Pempel 1998). To this end, the US provided financial and political support to the conservative Liberal Democratic Party (LDP) to keep socialists and communists out of power (Pempel 1998). The US also supported Japan's economic development through many preferential trade arrangements (Johnson 2004), while forcing other Asian nations and Okinawa to bear heavy military roles in the Cold War conflict, which hindered their economic development and democratisation (Li cited in Yoshimi 2007 p. 14).

70   Keita Takayama

In education, the US Occupation's democratising and demilitarising measures aimed to minimise the central control of the Ministry of Education (MoE) and to remove any remnants of the wartime imperial ideology from the education system. Many teachers who showed allegiance to the imperial regime were fired, and parts of school textbooks were blacked out to ensure that children were taught the values and ideologies consistent with the democratic and pacifist principles of 'new' Japan. The 1872 Imperial Rescript, which had played a key role in the spread of ultranationalism through education, was replaced in 1947 with the Fundamental Law of Education (FLE), which was to actualise in/through schools the democratic and pacifist principles of the new Constitution. Many of the systemic changes introduced during the occupation period were designed to distance political power from educational administration as a way to prevent a recurrence of the political indoctrination of the imperial past. This political intent was most clearly expressed in article X of the FLE: 'Education shall not be subject to improper control, but it shall be directly responsible to the whole people' (Horio 1988, p. 401). Guided by this principle, the Ministry's textbook screening – though it came to symbolise the unconstitutionality of state control over education in a series of legal cases in the subsequent decades – was introduced to keep the resurgence of militarism and totalitarianism in check (Morita 2011, p. 28). Likewise, the national course of study was introduced in 1947 not to straightjacket schools and teachers with prescribed curricular content, but simply to provide an overall curricular framework within which they were expected to exercise autonomy.

However, many of these measures were quickly reverted once the US became aware of the growing socialist movements and their strong influence in the newly instituted democratised education system. Indeed, socialists were gaining considerable political momentum before and after Japan's formal 'independence' from the US Occupation Regime in 1952. Socialist activists were elected to local school boards, while the Japan Teachers' Union, legalised in 1947 by the Occupation as part of its democratising measures (Shibata 2006, p. 97), was rapidly gaining political momentum in close association with the Socialist and Communist Parties (Oguma 2003). Many former Teachers' Union members successfully gained seats in the municipal and national parliaments as well on the local and prefectural school boards, constituting one of the key fractions within the Socialist Party (Takeuchi 2011, p. 196). Fearful of losing Japan – the US's capitalist model child – to the Communist bloc, the US government backed the regrouping of conservative political forces into the LDP in 1955. Then, the LDP, under strong US influence, reverted many of the newly instituted democratic mechanisms to strengthen the Ministry's political and administrative control. For instance, a set of laws was introduced to restrict teachers' political activities in 1954; the local school board election, introduced during the US Occupation, was terminated in 1956; and the national curriculum guideline became more prescriptive and legally binding in 1958.

Out of the political struggles against the 'reverse course' emerged the foundation of Japanese post-war politics, or what Hiroto Tahara (1996) terms the 'cold-war-era education scholarship' (*reisenki kyōikugaku*) (p. 4). The key characteristic

Towards de-cold-war politics 71

of this scholarship was the positioning of MoE and LDP as attempting to resuscitate the values and ideologies of Imperial Japan. Furthermore, it articulated the political motivations of the MoE and LDP to US imperialism, to which, they saw, the Japanese state played a subordinate role. The liberal-left struggle, led by the scholarship, was organised around the binary construct of citizens' freedom on the one hand and state power on the other and the protection of the former from the latter (Imai 1996; Morita 2011). Influenced by variants of Marxist ideology, education activists and scholars developed social movements around the notion of 'the people's right to education' (*kokumin no kyōiku ken*), which was diametrically opposed to the state's right to education. 'Never send children to the battlefield' was the slogan used to generate popular support at the time. As suggested by Naoto Morita (2011), the Marxist focus on class struggle was replaced with the 'people's' (*kokumin*) struggle against the state authority, a move which reflected the need to broaden the support base for the union-led movements at the time.

Eventually, the social movement, initially driven by Marxist activists and scholars, came to rely heavily on the liberal notion of neutrality of education (*kyōiku no chūritsu sei*) as a key rhetorical and legal device to challenge the 'reversing' changes (Hirota 2005; Imai 1996; Morita 2011; Tahara 1996). Informed by this development, the Teachers' Union and education scholars waged a series of court challenges over the teacher assessment scheme, the national scholastic assessments and the history textbook 'screening' in the 1960s and 1970s. Out of these extensive legal struggles emerged the unique conceptualisation of a public sphere in education, which is independent of state interference. It defined teachers as professionals entrusted with the democratic responsibilities of organising the people's (parents') private right to education, while the role of the state was restricted to the area of 'external conditioning for education' (*kōkyōiku no gaiteki jōken seibi*), guaranteeing teachers' complete autonomy over internal educational matters (curriculum and pedagogy). The binary positioning of 'private' versus 'state' became so pervasive during this period that any educational matters were reasoned and liberal-left struggles were waged in terms of this paradigm (Imai 1996).

Despite the critical role that the so-called 'cold-war-era education scholarship' played in keeping state control from education in earlier decades, it also created unwanted legacies that have been increasingly acknowledged by Japanese scholars over the last decades. As Yasuo Imai (1996) rightly points out, the alternative public sphere conceptualised by the movement never materialised in Japanese education from the 1970s onward. This was because its binary juxtaposition of private against state overlooked the historical complicity between them in Japanese education since its late nineteenth-century inception. Under the wartime imperial regime, for instance, people were not simply coerced or 'duped' into the ultra-nationalist ideology propagated by the 1872 Imperial Rescript. But the education system was designed to align individual aspiration for upward mobility with the regime's ideological project, hence people actively participated in the imperial project. The same channelling mechanism was soon formed in the 1960s and 1970s of Japan's rapid economic growth, during which universal access to

72 *Keita Takayama*

primary and secondary education was achieved (Kariya 1995). The highly competitive and yet egalitarian education system, formed by the late 1960s, allowed for people's pursuit of upward social mobility and better living standards to be closely tied to the state's overall economic agenda (Imai 1996, p. 157). Furthermore, the 'cold-war-era education scholarship' and the associated movement were vulnerable to the rise of neoliberalism in the 1990s, because the binary juxtaposition of private (individual freedom) and state control was reconciled by the neoliberal claims of achieving both individuality and freedom via choice, devolution on the one hand and control and order via 'responsibilisation' on the other (Ochi 2004).

Moreover, the 'sanctification' of political neutrality resulted in the depoliticisation of education in subsequent decades (Hirota 2015; Kodama 2012). As discussed earlier, the liberal-left legal battles against the LDP's 'reversing' measures resorted to the same liberal principle, making a constitutional case for preventing the MoE's interference in the 'internal' matters of education over which teachers were to enjoy complete autonomy. With some of the major court rulings endorsing this principle (in 1970, for instance), the separation of education from politics became part of the cold-war political settlement between the Right (LDP and MoE) and the Left (the Socialist Party and the Japan Teacher's Union). From then on, anything even remotely political was to be removed from what was to be taught. The depoliticisation of education was further reinforced in the 1960s and 1970s, according to Teruyuki Hirota (2015), during which high school students' involvement in radical political sects became a major social issue. In response, the MoE issued a number of ordinances to keep students out of political activities both in and outside of schools, contributing to the further separation of the school curriculum from anything potentially viewed as political. Hirota (2015) attributes this historical legacy to the poor state of civic education in Japan, where students simply memorise facts about democratic procedures and mechanisms, and to the deplorable level of civic attitude, skills and knowledge among Japanese middle school students. As will be discussed shortly, the same cold-war legacy continues to haunt the contemporary debate over nationalism in schools, the topic to which I now turn.

Controversy over the 'love of country'

Teaching 'love of country' has always been on the political agenda of the LDP, which remained in power for much of the post-war history, from its foundation in 1955 to the present. LDP conservative politicians saw the FLE and the Constitution as 'US impositions' and demanded the inclusion of moral values and responsibilities, including 'love of country', in the school curriculum. However, from the 1960s onward, the LDP shifted away from nationalistic politics and instead focused exclusively on achieving economic growth as the key ruling strategy. Since then, apart from outspoken nationalist politicians' occasional calls for patriotic teaching, such an explicit nationalist agenda fell out of the cold-war political settlement between the Right and Left. A political consensus was formed that teaching 'love of country' violates the principle of neutrality, and the MoE knew that pursuing it would bring the Ministry into unwanted legal battles with the Teachers' Union and liberal-left education scholars (see Takayama 2010 for a more detailed discussion on this history).

It was only in the late 1990s that teaching 'love of country' emerged as a legitimate policy agenda. Indeed, during this period, many programs and policies were introduced to reinforce Japanese national identity. For instance, the 1999 legal change made it mandatory for schools to ensure that the national flag (*hinomaru*) is hoisted and the anthem (*kimigayo*) is sung at school events.[1] The early 2000s distribution of supplementary moral education material, *kokoro no nōto* (notebook for heart), was also criticised for promoting students' romantic identification with the country (Irie 2004). But the most controversial of all was the proposed revision to the 1947 FLE, which was ratified in 2006 after lengthy parliamentary and public debates and a series of political skirmishes (see Takayama 2008 for details). The LDP proposed that the law be revised to include such phrases as 'pride as Japanese', 'identity as Japanese', 'love of home town and country', 'respect for tradition and culture' and 'public spirit' as the key moral values to be taught in schools.

Many liberal-left education scholars explain this sudden nationalistic turn in terms of its link to the drastic 'regime shift' of the time that resulted in increasing economic and social risk and disparity (Hirota 2005, 2009; Nishihara 2003; Ōuchi 2003; Sanuki 2003). The radical structural reform of the time disrupted the set of political and economic mechanisms that had given people a sense of belonging and economic stability. Neoliberal social and economic reform, beginning in the late 1990s, created a widening disparity in society, undermining the metanarrative of post-war economic nationalism where a sense of 'us' was secured through various developmentalist state policies, including a comprehensive range of egalitarian measures in education (Kariya 1995). Furthermore, it also corresponded to the increasing flows of migrants and transnationalisation of Japanese corporations and civil society at the time, which considerably blurred the imagined sense of national community. The call for teaching 'love of country' and Japanese identity in schools hence reflects the desire of the state apparatus to offset the increasing fragmentation of an imagined sense of community, in political, economic and cultural terms.

Predictably, the liberal-left critique of the proposed FLE revision draws heavily upon the legacy of the cold-war-era education scholarship and its social movement. For instance, Hiroshi Sanuki (2003) argues that the proposed inclusion of moral values, as in the inclusion of the phrase 'Japanese with rich heart and strong will', violates the liberal principle of the law that rejects the subordination of individuality to state authority. He also problematises the proposed stress on 'Japanese identity', arguing that it excludes ethnic Korean and Chinese permanent residents who do not have Japanese nationality. Likewise, Tetsuya Takahashi (2003, p. 13) maintains that the proposed emphasis on 'love of country' and 'Japanese identity' is designed to render education a key device with which the state attempts to nurture 'national consciousness' which it sees as necessary for possible wars in the future. Hence, in his mind, the FLE revision was meant to justify people's ultimate sacrifice to the cause of the state (Takahashi 2004, p. 71).

74   *Keita Takayama*

Similarly, Yōichi Komori (2004) argues that the purpose of the FLE revision is to enable Japan to wage wars, breaking away from Japan's pacifist tradition underpinned by Constitution Article 9.[2] Other critics, such as Yōko Irie (2004), Kōichirō Komikawa (2004) and Hirokazu Ōuchi (2004), make a similar critique about the revision, stressing the danger and unconstitutionality of state intervention in children's conscience. Ōuchi (2004) agrees with Takahashi that the proposed inclusion of 'love of country' is designed to prepare children for sacrifice to the cause of the country. All these scholars, therefore, see the FLE revision as a step towards making Japan a 'normal country', removing the constitutional constraints on the country's military activities. As an attempt to highlight the dangerous nationalistic trend that the proposed revision sets in motion, all these scholars associate it to the 1872 Imperial Rescript.

Teruyuki Hirota (2005), on the other hand, distances himself from those who link the proposed revision to the legacy of past militarism. He warns that the proposed stress on 'Japanese identity' could promote ethnocentrism in Japan, while at the same time excluding ethnic minority students in Japanese schools. Hirota fears that it could also negatively affect Japan's international relations, as he sees the revision as 'closed and inward-looking', potentially isolating Japan from the rest of Asia, where people are highly sensitive about Japan's nationalism due to their direct experience of its wartime aggression. He goes on to argue that Japan is a country full of 'love of country' (p. 179); because of a relative lack of cultural, linguistic and 'racial' diversity, Japanese students are much more exposed than those in other countries to positive messages about their country's tradition and culture, both through the subject-specific curriculum (literacy, history and social studies) and through media events. Given that growing up and being schooled in Japan already provides ample opportunities to develop national consciousness and that the renewed stress on 'love of country' could easily worry neighbouring Asian countries, he sees little point in its proposed inclusion in the revised FLE.

In sum, three key characteristics can be identified in these liberal-left critics' arguments. First, they show strong aversion to the stress on 'Japanese' as an identity marker. Here, they tend to treat 'Japanese' as an ethnic marker, hence seeing the proposed stress on Japanese identity as premised upon the myth of cultural homogeneity (Befu 2001). They argue that the references to 'our country's tradition and culture' in the proposed revision are exclusionary and discriminatory, as they do not include 'other' (marginalised) traditions and cultures within Japan. Second, they closely associate the proposed revision with the wartime imperial past and militarism and consequently reject any attempt to nurture national identity through schooling. Third, they see nationalism and cosmopolitanism as necessarily incompatible, assuming that promotion of the former undermines the latter (consider Hirota's concern about Japan's isolation in Asia, for instance). By and large, therefore, these scholars continue to operate within the discourse of cold-war politics wherein the thesis of political neutrality rules out any possibility of nurturing national sentiment through education. Clearly, the 'ghost' of the imperialist past (Ochi 2004, p. 137) – or the 'legacy of the cold-war-era education scholarship' (Tahara 1996, p. 4) – continues to cast a spell on how nationalism is articulated in the political discourse of Japanese education today.

Nationalism, democracy and education

The cold-war 'neutrality' principle has prevented liberal-left scholars and activists from exploring the place of nationalism in schools. Consequently, the Japanese educational discourse of nationalism has been completely monopolised by the romanticism of the political right, including the Shinzō Abe Cabinet (2007-present), which sees some, if not all, aspects of the Imperial Rescript as means to 'revive Japan'. Then, the task is not to engage in the kind of oppositional politics that have rendered the leftist and liberal struggle purely reactionary and oppositional, but to unlearn the 'neutrality' thesis and recognise the essentially political nature of education. Shigeo Kodama (2012) takes his cues from Luis Althusser's work in taking Japanese politics of education beyond the cold-war legacy. Drawing upon his notion of relative autonomy, he argues that education is part of the state apparatus, whose ideological effect is never predetermined. He calls for looking at education as an inherently political sphere within which given power relations are already embedded, thus refuting the idea of 'removing politics from education' (see also Imai 1996). Education is part of social processes through which new political subjectivities can emerge and be made and remade, or what Gert Biesta (2010) calls 'subjectification' (24). Strategies taking this view seriously should focus on politics of re-articulation, which could result in contradictory and often unpredictable subjectifying effects.

Indeed, nationalism can serve different functions and purposes, both democratic and undemocratic. And yet, by and large, nationalism has been viewed as something bad. It is often associated with the extreme human atrocities committed by Nazi Germany, Imperial Japan and ethnocentric genocide in Africa and Eastern Europe, for instance. It was only in the last decade or two that a more careful assessment of nationalism has begun to highlight its positive aspects, including its constitutive role for democracy, redistributive politics and social cohesion (e.g., Miller 1995; Tamir 1993). This body of literature hence serves as a caution against the deconstructive critique of nationalism inspired by Benedict Anderson's (1991) work on 'imagined community'. As Toshihito Kayano (2005) points out, humans as social beings always require some sense of belonging and identity formed within a shared social space, no matter how fabricated it might be. Certainly recognising the inherently fabricated nature of social relations is important because it allows us to imagine it differently. But it does not negate the fact that humans will require some sense of belonging and that nation-states will continue to be one of the significant, if not the only, sources for human identity (White 1997). Furthermore, Sang-jung Kang (2006, pp. 186–187), drawing on Masao Maruyama, argues that integral to nationalism is the dialectical tension between loyalty and rebellion (see also Oguma 2003). The sense of being restrained by the national community in turn constitutes the internal source of energy for rebellion. Indeed, David Miller (1995) sees national bonding as fundamental to the realisation of redistributive justice. Redistributive social policies gain political legitimacy only when people's emotional bonds with those in need 'outweigh narrower considerations of their personal gains and losses' (White 1996, p. 331). Hence, national sentiment constitutes the emotional basis

76   *Keita Takayama*

for collective political rebellion when a state acts in violation of the rights of the people under its governance.

All of these suggest that nationalism can become the source of collective identity, which can be channelled to protect what is public in the age of aggressive neoliberal social and economic reform. The task is then not just to deconstruct the imagined sense of national belonging, nor is it to remain haunted by the 'ghost of the imperial past'. Rather, it is to see the 'political benefit' (White 1996, p. 331) in reconstituting nationalism towards more desirable social and political ends (Miller 1995; White 1997, 1996). This insight relates to the feminist work around the strategic use of essentialism. Just as femininity was constructed as 'women's essence', which was then mobilised towards the feminist liberation movements, the imagined sense of national community can be appropriated towards given political ends. The sort of crucial questions to be explored in this strategic engagement with nationalism would be 'for whose struggle and what political ends and under what circumstance is it being pursued?' (Motohashi 2007, p. 149).

Indeed, nationalism assumes contradictory functions with vastly different political consequences. On the one hand, political theorists are rightly cautious of the exclusionary and discriminatory forces that the unqualified loyalty to state – 'My country, right or wrong' – can create (Gutmann 1999, p. 312). Indeed, human history is full of examples where state power mobilised national sentiment constituted on the basis of 'race', ethnicity, culture and language to justify human atrocities against 'others' both within and outside the nation-state. While fully aware of this danger, however, political theorists also recognise the constitutive roles of nationalism for developing people's commitment to democratic polity. As Craig Calhoun (2002) maintains, 'democracy has depended on national identities to a greater degree than many critics of nationalism recognise' (151).

As an attempt to distinguish elements of nationalism that are conducive to democracy from those that are not, scholars in political philosophy have developed distinctions between ethnic and civic nationalism. Ethnic nationalism represents a sense of national belonging based on the 'inheritance' of shared culture, ethnicity, language and tradition. As membership in this imagined community is defined in terms of shared ethnicity, culture and language, it could promote ethnocentrism and discrimination, violating the liberal principles of freedom, justice and equality. Aesthetic and emotional language dominates this discourse, potentially promoting blind loyalty to the nation-state (Kang 2006). On the other hand, civic nationalism represents a sense of national belonging based on allegiance to civic virtues that the nation-state supposedly represents. Political – as opposed to aesthetic and emotional – language dominates its discourse, hence keeping a healthy distance from the possible violence of ethnic nationalism.

However, the binary distinction between reason (social contract) and emotion in the conceptualisation of nationalism has been critiqued by other political theorists. David Miller (1995) and Will Kymlicka (1999, 1995) question whether shared commitment to civic virtues is a sufficient foundation for a shared political identity, solidarity and loyalty, which they see as fundamental to citizens' democratic commitment. Kymlicka argues that 'the idea of a purely non-cultural definition of civic nationalism is implausible' (p. 200) and hence that shared values (including affirmation of cultural diversity), language and culture play an indisputable role in the constitution of national sentiment, the collective sense of 'us'. Likewise, Maurizio Viroli (1995) questions the same distinction and argues that elements of ethnic nationalism are always present in liberal democratic states that endorse the civic form of nationalism. He argues that liberal polity necessitates what he calls the 'alchemy of passions' (p. 10) – conversion of an emotional sense of belonging developed through shared language, culture and history into allegiance to civic virtues and democratic principles.

In critiquing recent theoretical development around constitutional patriotism and cosmopolitanism, Calhoun (2002) addresses the same contradiction between nationalism and democracy. He argues that much of the theoretical work is underpinned by the image of 'bad nationalism', the fear of 'ethnic solidarity that triumphs over civility and liberal values and ultimately turns to horrific violence' (p. 150). Then he goes on to argue that Jürgen Habermas's notion of constitutional patriotism is premised upon a problematic notion of culture as 'inheritance' and peoplehood as 'a matter of some pre-established, passive cultural affinity' (p. 155). This is why, argues Calhoun, Habermas focuses on the proper procedure and legal frameworks for rational deliberation, assuming that the public sphere constituted as such will 'produce a rational agreement that can take the place of pre-established culture as the basis for political identity' (p. 155). Calhoun questions the notion of peoplehood as pre-political, arguing that this will only create a decidedly thin sense of 'the people' and mutual commitment. Then he calls for the notion of culture as 'activity' and peoplehood as 'the potential result of an active process of public engagement' (p. 155), that is, peoplehood as something to be made and remade through participation in democratic public life. Hence, he rejects Habermas's artificial separation of reason from culture and sees political process as integral to the emerging sense of peoplehood.

The possible role of education for national sentiment has been debated in a manner paralleling the larger theoretical discussion reviewed above. According to David Archard (1999), the debate centres on the tension between the liberal underpinning of education and patriotism. That is, 'the liberal polity requires that its citizens patriotically identify with one another and with the project which that polity represents. Yet, if we teach patriotism civic education betrays the ideals which, arguably, are constitutive of any proper education, chiefly a commitment to the standards of critical reason' (p. 167). Archard takes the view that it is impossible for schools to nurture patriotism without compromising on its liberal principle of critical reasoning. Furthermore, he maintains that national identity is 'one element of an (sic) heterogeneous identity' and it need not be the most important element' (p. 170). Such a view is challenged by John White (1996), who sees it as an important function of schools to develop national sentiment. To him, national unity on the basis of allegiance to civic principles is not sufficient for democratic polity and needs to be complemented with a 'more spontaneous, less intellectualised kind of sentiment' (p. 332). Likewise, Walter Feinberg (1998) cautions how race/ethnicity-based identity politics can undermine the shared sense of national belonging, which he sees as fundamental to

78 *Keita Takayama*

democratic commitment. Hence, he recognises it as the role of what he calls 'common schools' to develop the skills and attitudes conducive to the development of a shared national identity.

Such a defence of schooling for national sentiment has been challenged by those who call for cosmopolitan education, however. Martha Nussbaum (1996), for instance, is concerned that the sense of national belonging is being developed to the exclusion of identification with and compassion for those who reside outside the national borders. She argues that 'the defence of shared national values . . . requires appealing to certain basic features of human personhood that obviously also transcend national boundaries' (p. 6). Hence, she calls for shifting away from schools' primary focus on domestic politics, tradition and history to develop students' cosmopolitan compassion and imagination. In response, Amy Gutmann (1999) argues that the kind of moral obligations of citizenship developed through what she calls democratic education 'do not stop at state boundaries' (p. 315). She justifies democratic education's disproportionate focus on domestic matters as due to logistics (there is too much to cover in the school curriculum) and because domestic matters have greater relevance for students. This, however, does not mean that the history, culture and politics of other countries can be neglected. The key is not to see national commitment and cosmopolitanism as in a zero-sum relationship, but to recognise the coexistence of ethnic, national and cosmopolitan identities in each student and develop their commitments to the identities with which they identify. However, given that the nation-state remains one of the most significant arenas where key political decisions are made with considerable implications for the lives of people both within and beyond a given country, schools need to recognise national identity as one of the most crucial identifications that they are to nurture (Feinberg 1998; Gutmann 1999).

To summarise, much of the existing debate around nationalism and democracy and the role of schools in this relationship has been guided by the need to find 'the functional equivalent of the ethnic nation' (Calhoun 2002, p. 153). The careful discriminating work of nationalism is underpinned by the acknowledgement that the 'manners for love of country' assumes considerably different political meanings depending on which definition of nationalism is adopted (Kang 2006). It is the affective requirement of democracy that warrants a role of nationalism in its development. As pointed out by Chantal Mouffe (cited in Biesta 2011), the 'desire for democracy' cannot be taught, but 'can only be fuelled' through affective means (p. 152). The real challenge for democratic politics is how we can mobilise people's passions – anger, empathy and sympathy – towards democratic designs. Nationalism is surely one of the, if not the only, powerful sources of passions – 'one of the moving forces in the field of politics' (Mouffe 2005, p. 24) – that could be capitalised upon for vibrant democracy. Unfortunately, the discourse of nationalism in Japan has been overshadowed by the 'ghost of the imperial past'; it has been dominated by the Right, who articulate nationalism in the cultural, emotive and aesthetic language reminiscent of the imperial past, and by the Left, who associate any call for national sentiment with the ethnocentrism and militarism of the past. What gets lost in the midst of all this is a much-needed attempt to work out the possible roles that schools can play for the 'alchemy of passions': transforming national sentiment into the desire for democracy.

This problem is most clearly demonstrated in Hirota's (2005) argument that there is no need to teach 'love of country' in schools because Japanese students already have a strong emotional attachment to and identification with their country. He is not alone here, as other scholars also point to the prevalence of cultural nationalism in Japan disseminated widely through the popular genre called *nihonjinron*, or theories/discussions about the Japanese (see Befu 2001; Takayama 2011). His argument, however, fails to discriminate between the different functions and ends of nationalism. As a result, he rules out any potential roles that schools can play in channelling the national sentiment into students' commitment to the desire for democracy. This is a significant omission, because, according to Hirota (2005, 2015), Japanese youths, compared to those in other countries, have a much higher level of national sentiment and pride on the one hand and a deplorable level of civic skills, knowledge and attitude on the other. Seen from the perspective developed above, it could be argued that the lack of concerted effort to perform the 'alchemy of passions' through schooling might explain, at least partly, the relative lack of civility among Japanese students. By attributing the latter to the 'neutrality' problem of post-war Japanese education and its depoliticising effect on the school curriculum, Hirota (2005, 2015) falls short of exploring the possible missing link between strong national sentiment and low civic mindedness among Japanese youths.

However, what should be problematised further in the debate over the role of schooling for national sentiments is the static conception of culture, nationhood and subjectivity that both the proponents and their critics tend to accept. As suggested by Calhoun and Biesta, it is through the processes of participation in democratic polity that new political and national subjectivities can emerge. Likewise, culture and peoplehood are to be made and remade through people's participation in democratic processes, suggesting that their national and civic identities are not fully shaped before their participation in deliberation. Biesta (2011) rightly points out, drawing on Jacques Rancière, that 'establishing oneself as a subject does not take place before the 'act' of politics but rather in and through it' (p. 149). It is through political processes of deliberation that people learn to question the very border separating 'us and them' and learn to redraw the political and national boundaries (Biesta 2011). This insight allows us to question the view of schooling as an agent that socialises students into existing orders of things, the view on which much of the discussion around nationalism in schools is premised; the debate is centred on whether or not teaching for a particular prefabricated national identity is compatible with the liberal principle of education. The notions of culture, peoplehood and student subjectivity are political concepts that defy any prefabricating attempt to fix them beforehand. This reconceptualisation helps shift our attention away from the narrow focus on what to teach (e.g., whose history do we teach?) to how to teach, and how the overall educational experience should be arranged so that students are sufficiently exposed to the kinds of activities and deliberating experiences that facilitate the making and remaking of their civic and national subjectivities.

80 *Keita Takayama*

So far, I have explored multiple functions of nationalism and its complex relationship with democracy and the possible mediating roles that schools can play for the 'alchemy of passions'. Particular stress has been placed on the role of schooling in providing learning opportunities that facilitate the emergence of new civic and national identities that are constantly made and remade. Needless to say, the strategic mobilisation of nationalism for the purposes of redistributive justice and thick democracy must be done thoughtfully: it needs to be carefully disarticulated from the two closely related regressive political discourses of the time. First is the neoliberal discourse of responsibilisation; nationalistic sentiment is mobilised as part of its moralising discourse wherein structural causes of social disorder and risk are individualised (Ochi 2004). Second is the discourse of ethnic nationalism that can lead to dangerous ethnic chauvinism and ethnocentrism. These cautionary points will inform how the de-cold-war politics can be enacted in order to channel the rising nationalist force in today's context of Japanese education towards a more just and equitable society, the focus of the next section.

Enacting de-cold-war politics

One of the most contested aspects of the revision to the 1947 FLE was the inclusion of the following phrases: 'pride as Japanese', 'identity as Japanese', 'love of home town and country', 'respect for tradition and culture' and 'public spirit'. These terms clearly reflect the conservative politics characterised by the romantic desire for the collectivist – including imperial – past and the cultural homogeneity of the people. As Hirota (2005) rightly points out, the identity marker 'Japanese' has been used in the country's education policy discourse to implicitly exclude ethnic minority permanent residents of Japan (e.g., ethnic Koreas and Chinese and the Japanese Indigenous Ainu people). Hence, it is certainly legitimate to fear that the proposed stress on 'Japanese pride and identity' could hinder any progress in the politics of cultural recognition.

However, these phrases are open to various rearticulations. For instance, the term 'Japanese' can be rearticulated not as an ethnic/racial/nationality marker that excludes 'others' on these grounds, but as a country-specific marker for civic commitment within which multiple cultural identities are placed and celebrated. Here, the shared cultural identity is indeed 'singular' (Archard 1999, p. 170) and yet never totalising nor static. Following Calhoun's (2002) earlier discussion of 'culture' and 'peoplehood', the shared cultural identity is not a pre-political concept, but it is something that continues to be made and remade through 'an active process of public engagement' (p. 155). When national identity is conceptualised in such a dynamic fashion, the stress on Japanese identity no longer leads to the kind of exclusionary politics of difference based on the homogeneity myth of Japan. Here, Japanese identity and pride are no longer conditioned by ascribed characteristics such as ethnicity and nationality but expressed through civic commitment; 'active interest and participation in the polity to which one belongs' (Junichi Saito, cited in Hirota 2005, p. 154). As Walter Feinberg (1998) argues in the US context, one of the central democratic roles of 'common schools' is to serve as a site for the making and remaking of the shared national identity and commitment which embrace students' 'uncommon' (diverse) identities. Hence, ethnic minorities are not to be socialised into the existing national identity, which remains fixed (see Biesta's [2010] discussion of 'socialisation'); rather, they are to be recognised as an active, co-constructing agent of a shared, constantly evolving national identity.

This reconceptualisation of national identity presents an important pedagogic implication because it demands that schools provide opportunities for 'an active process of public engagement' whereby a share sense of 'us' is to be constantly negotiated. Here, the emphasis is placed on the pedagogic process of what Biesta (2010) calls 'subjectification', 'the promotion of a kind of citizenship that is not merely about the reproduction of a predefined template but that takes political agency seriously' (p. 24). Students' commitment to a multi-ethnic Japan can be nurtured and their shared sense of identity constantly reconstituted through participating in collective deliberation and decision making over matters that affect multicultural communities across the country. Unfortunately, by criticising the proposed stress on 'Japanese pride and identity' on the basis of the 'common sense' interpretation of being Japanese (peoplehood as a pre-political concept), the aforementioned Japanese critics fail to capitalise upon the generative potentials of rearticulation work for an emerging national identity. In so doing, they withdraw themselves from the cultural politics over these highly contestable nationalistic concepts.

Likewise, many of the Japanese critics criticise the inclusion of 'love of hometown and country' in the school assessment criteria in the city of Fukuoka in southern Japan (see Hirota 2005; Nishihara 2003). The criteria under their scrutiny state that students should be assessed on their ability 'to embrace our country's tradition and history and love of country, while developing consciousness as Japanese in the world who wish for peace'. To these liberal-left critics, the assessment criteria exemplify the dangerous penetration of a nationalistic agenda at the local school level and suggest what is to come once the FLE revision is ratified. But once again, 'history', 'tradition' and 'embrace' can be disarticulated from the discourse of ethnic nationalism and into civic nationalism, where Japan's tradition of pacifism, democracy and civic activism, which the critics fear that the FLE revision furthermore marginalises (e.g., Irie 2004, p. 210), is foregrounded. This 'national tradition' was most recently exemplified in September 2015 in the mass demonstration of 120,000 people against the controversial new military laws proposed by the Abe Cabinet.

Indeed, the 'tradition' and 'history' of Japan do not at all have to be those reflecting the 'selective tradition' of the government or the dominant ethnic group. The current conservative government has aggressively attempted to remove references to Japan's war crimes from school textbooks, arguing that the 'masochistic' history deprives children of national pride (see Takayama and Apple 2008). Against this political context, the liberal-left critics fear that the assessment criteria in Fukuoka further force teachers to move away from teaching about the darker aspects of Japan's past. However, the reference in the criteria – 'our country's tradition and history' – does not specify which/whose tradition and history of Japan it refers to. Hence, for instance, Japan's modern history can be looked at from multiple perspectives of Asian 'others' both within and outside Japan. Such historical accounts would necessarily include references to Korean and Chinese residents' struggles for justice and equality and Japan's wartime aggression against its Asian neighbours, including reference to the issue of 'comfort women'[3] that the current Abe government has successfully removed from its approved textbooks. Being exposed to multiple ways of looking at contested historical events, students will come to understand the essentially political nature of what counts as history, textbook and school knowledge in general. It is through such pedagogy of rearticulation that students engage in the collective processes of making and remaking an inclusive sense of national identity that is open to domestic diversity as well as to the perspectives beyond the national boundaries. Here, national commitment and cosmopolitanism are not in a zero-sum relationship, but can be simultaneously pursued.

All of this rearticulating work is still 'patriotic', because 'whatever version of national history is taught, whether the bright side or the dark side, reinforces the idea of one's nation as morally worthy' (White 1997, p. 21). Furthermore, the sanitised version of national history can become a cause of national disunity, according to Kymlicka (1999, p. 97), because any historical account that ignores the state's oppression of minorities and women and their struggles for justice alienates them from the collective sense of national belonging. He sees history teaching as a particularly important means of developing students' emotional identification with their country, 'one of the few means available to maintain social unity in a pluralistic state' (p. 97). Here it must be noted that White's and Kymlicka's insights, which tend to focus on what to teach (e.g., whose histories?), are somehow limited in that they rest on the uncomplicated notion of the 'effect' of particular history teaching on students' national identity, whereby the inclusion of minoritised histories in the national narrative is presumed to create a unified national identity among students. Here, a particular desirable conception of national identity is presupposed and history teaching is viewed as a means to helping students 'acquire it', as opposed to the view of history teaching as part of overall educational arrangements where student subjectivities are made and remade through democratic participation. In sum, I have suggested how educators can rearticulate the concepts, which have long been associated with 'bad' nationalism, for deeper public engagement through which what it means to be Japanese in the world is constantly reconstituted. When this is effectively done, what the national flag – now legally required to be hoisted at important school events across the country – could represent to Japanese students might be radically different from what the liberal-left critics fear.

Towards Asia as method

The spell of cold-war politics has long haunted the articulation of nationalism in Japanese education. The principle of 'neutrality', which has guided liberal-left politics for the last several decades, has prevented any serious exploration of the strategic uses of nationalism for further advancing democratic commitment. As a result, the language of nationalism has become the exclusive property of the political Right, and no serious attempt has been made to consider the legitimate place of nationalism in the school curriculum. Against this background, I have attempted to reclaim nationalism from the conservative monopoly, and in so doing, have tried to shake off the dead weight of cold-war politics from the discussion of 'love of country' in Japanese education.

Indeed, many Japanese scholars recognise the depoliticising effect of the cold-war legacy and call for various strategies for the repoliticisation of the school curriculum and youths (see Hirota 2009, 2015; Kodama 2012, 2013). However, curiously, none of these scholars see nationalism as a potential resource for repoliticisation, an attempt to bring politics back into the classroom. In this sense, their de-cold-war politics remains partial because they have fallen short of 'reopen(ing) the past for reflection in order to make moments of liberation possible in the future' (Chen 2010, p. x). As a way to release us from the cold-war spell and to demonstrate how the de-cold-war politics might be enacted in schools, I have discussed politics of rearticulation whereby the conservative call for inculcating national sentiment through schooling can be rearticulated into a democratic discourse so that the same nationalistic force can serve a radically different political end.

The analysis presented in this chapter can be situated as part of the larger transformation of knowledge structure and subjectivity in Asia that Chen (2010) advocates. More specifically, the chapter contributes towards what he proposes as a strategy for the de-cold-war politics, 'Asia as method', the term he uses after Yoshimi Takeuchi. With this, he means that 'using the idea of Asia as an imaginary anchoring point, societies in Asia can become each other's points of reference, so that the understanding of the self may be transformed, and subjectivity rebuilt' (p. 212). For this to take place, scholars in Asia need to reflect upon how the US-driven cold-war politics have not merely conditioned 'our identities but has become deeply embedded within our subjectivity' in Asia (p. 178). It is hoped that as more and more scholars based in or attached to Asia attempt to disrupt the cold-war spell on politics of education and possible subjectivities constituted through its pedagogic processes, we will move closer to the formation of multiplying reference points in and for Asia, the condition that Chen deems essential for the emergence of new political subjectivities and imaginations in the region.

Notes

1 Singing the national anthem and hoisting the national flag remain highly contested in Japanese education. Since they were made mandatory in 1999, there have been numerous lawsuits filed by union teachers and education scholars who deem the act to be in violation of constitutional rights to freedom of thought and conscience.
2 The Constitution's Preamble and Article 9 proclaim that Japan has resolved not to become a military power and not to pose a military threat to other nations.
3 'Comfort women' euphemistically refers to the enslaved women who were forced to sexually serve the Japanese military. Between 1932 and 1945, thousands of women, mostly from China, Korea and the Philippines, were rounded up and imprisoned in so-called 'comfort stations' (*ianjo*) – brothels – where they were repeatedly raped by Japanese military personnel.

84 Keita Takayama

References

Anderson, B. (1991). *Imagined communities: Reflections on the origin and spread of nationalism.* London: Verso.

Archard, D. (1999). Should we teach patriotism? *Studies in Philosophy and Education* 18: 157–173.

Befu, H. (2001). *Hegemony of homogeneity: An anthropological analysis of nihonjinron.* Melbourne: Trans Pacific Press.

Biesta, G. (2010). *Good education in an age of measurement: Ethics, politics, democracy.* London: Paradigm Publisher.

Biesta, G. (2011). The ignorant citizen: Mouffe, Rancière, and the subject of democratic education. *Studies in Philosophy and Education* 30(2): 141–153.

Calhoun, C. (2002). Imagining solidarity: Cosmopolitanism, constitutional patriotism, and the public sphere. *Public Culture* 14(1): 147–171.

Chen, K. (2010). *Asia as method: Toward de-imperialization.* Durham: Duke University Press.

Feinberg, W. (1998). *Common schools/uncommon identities: National unity and cultural difference.* New Haven, CT: Yale University Press.

Gutmann, A. (1999). *Democratic education.* Princeton, NJ: Princeton University Press.

Hirota, T. (2005). *Aikoku shin no yukue: Kyōiku kihonhō kaisei toiu mondai* [Where would the love of country go?: The problem of FLE revision]. Tokyo: Serashobō.

Hirota, T. (2009). *Kakusa/Chitsujo fuan to kyōiku* [Disparity/fear for disorder and education]. Tokyo: Sera Shoten.

Hirota, T. (2015). *Kyōiku wa nanio subekika: Nōryoku, shokugyō and shimin* [What education should do: Capability, jobs and citizens]. Tokyo: Iwanami shoten.

Horio, T. (1988). *Educational thought and ideology in modern Japan.* Tokyo: University of Tokyo Press.

Imai, Y. (1996). Miushinawareta kōkyōsei o motomete [In search of the idea of the public: Some discussions in the Japanese post-war education]. *History of Educational Thought Society* 5: 149–165.

Irie, Y. (2004). *Kyōkasho ga abunai* [Dangerous textbooks]. Tokyo: Iwanami shoten.

Johnson, C.A. (2004). *Blowback.* New York: Henry Holt and Co.

Kang, S. (2006). *Aikoku no sahō* [Manners for love of country]. Tokyo: Asahi shobo.

Kariya, T. (1995). *Taishū kyōiku shakai no yukue* [The future of mass education society]. Tokyo: Chūkō shinsho.

Kayano, T. (2005). *Kokka towa nanika* [What is state?]. Tokyo: Ibunsha.

Kodama, S. (2012). Toward the politics of education: Focusing on the post-Althusserian conception of ideology [in Japanese]. *Japan Academic Society for Educational Policy* 18: 8–17.

Kodama, S. (2013). Kokka to kyōiku ni okeru seijitekinaru monono ichika [Positional value of politics in the relationship between state and education]. *Kyōiku tetsugaku kenkyū* 107: 42–48.

Komikawa, K. (2004). Kitaisareru ningenzō no sakeme: Kyōiku kihonhō kaisei mondai ni yosete [A crack in the desired image of humans: On the problem of the FLE revision]. *Gendai shisō* 32(4): 93–103.

Komori, Y. (2004). Kihonhōkaiaku to sensō wo suru kuni [Evil revision of FLE and a country waging wars]. *Gendai shisō* 32(4): 78–88.

Kymlicka, W. (1995). *Multicultural citizenship.* Oxford: Clarendon Press.

Kymlicka, W. (1999). Education for citizenship. In M. Halstead and T. McLaughlin (Eds.), *Education in morality* (pp. 79–102). London: Routledge.

Miller, D. (1995). *On nationality.* Oxford: Clarendon Press.

Towards de-cold-war politics 85

Morita, N. (2011). The Ienaga textbook court cases revisited: A case analysis of an ideological controversy [in Japanese]. *Nihon kyōiku seisaku gakkai nenpō* 18: 18–39.

Motohashi, T. (2007). *Posuto koroniarizumu* [Postcolonialism] Tokyo: Iwanami shoten.

Mouffe, C. (2005). *On the political.* Abingdon and New York: Routledge.

Nishihara, H. (2003). *Gakkō ga aikokushin o oshierutoki* [When schools teach love of country]. Tokyo: Nihon hyōronsha.

Nussbaum, M. (1996). Patriotism and Cosmopolitanism. In J. Cohen (Ed.), *For love of country* (pp. 3–20). New York: Beacon Press.

Ochi, Y. (2004). Kyōiku to neo riberarizumu: Sengokyōiku no wana karano dasshutsu ni mukete [Education and neoliberalism: Escaping from the trap of the post-war education discourse]. In S. Tanaka (Ed.), *Kyōiku no kyōseitai e* [Body educational] (pp. 135–154). Tokyo: Tōshindō.

Oguma, E. (2003). *Minshū to aikoku* [Democracy and patriotism]. Tokyo: Shinyōsha.

Ōuchi, H. (2003). *Kyōiku kihonhō kaiseiron hihan* [A critique of the revision to the Fundamental Law of Education]. Tokyo: Hakutaku sha.

Ōuchi, H. (2004). Kyōiku wa dareno mono nanoka [Who is education for?]. *Gendai shisō* 32(4): 90–92.

Pempel, T.J. (1998). *Regime shift.* Ithaca, NY: Cornell University Press.

Sanuki, H. (2003). *Shinjuyūshigi to kyōiku kaikaku* [Neoliberalism and education reform]. Tokyo: Shunpōsha.

Shibata, M. (2006). Education, national identity and religion in Japan in an age of globalization. In D. Coulby and E. Zambeta (Eds.), *World yearbook of education: Globalization and nationalism in education* (pp. 89–113). Abingdon: RoutledgeFalmer.

Tahara, H. (1996). Kihanronteki kyōikuron no kiro [Normative education theory at a crossroad]. *Sapporo daigaku sōgō ronsou* 2: 1–10.

Takahashi, T. (2003). *Kokoro to sensō* [Heart and war]. Tokyo: Shōbunsha.

Takahashi, T. (2004). Kokumin kyōiku to gisei no porittikkusu [Education for the nationals and politics of sacrifice]. *Gendai shisō* 32(4): 70–77.

Takayama, K. (2008). Japan's Ministry of Education 'becoming the right': Neoliberal restructuring and the ministry's struggles for political legitimacy. *Globalisation, Societies, and Education* 6(2): 131–146.

Takayama, K. (2010). From the rightist 'coup' to the new beginning of progressive politics in Japanese education. In M.W. Apple (Ed.), *Global crises, social justice, and education* (pp. 61–111). New York: Routledge.

Takayama, K. (2011). Other Japanese educations and Japanese education otherwise. *Asia Pacific Journal of Education* 31(3): 345–359.

Takayama, K. and Apple, M.W. (2008). The cultural politics of borrowing: Japan, Britain, and the narrative of educational crisis. *British Journal of Sociology of Education* 29(3): 289–301.

Takeuchi, Y. (2011). *Kakushin gensō no sengoshi* [Post-war history of progressives' illusion]. Tokyo: Chūō kōron shinsha.

Tamir, Y. (1993). *Liberal nationalism.* Princeton, NJ: Princeton University Press.

Viroli, M. (1995). *For love of country: An essay on patriotism and nationalism.* Oxford: Clarendon Press.

White, J. (1996). Education and nationality. *Journal of Philosophy of Education* 30(3): 327–343.

White, J. (1997). National myths, democracy and education. In D. Bridges (Ed.), *Education, autonomy and democratic citizenship* (pp. 15–35). London: Routledge.

Yoshimi, Y. (2007). *Shinbei to hanbei: Sengo nihon no seijiteki muishiki* [Pro-US and anti-US: Political unconsciousness in post-war Japan]. Tokyo: Iwanami shoten.

6 Post-political governing of welfare state education in Sweden

Rita Foss Lindblad and Sverker Lindblad

What is the case?

In a live television newscast in the late spring of 2015, OECD experts invited by the Swedish government presented their report on education in Sweden. The report was summarised on the OECD's website (2015–05–04):

> Sweden has failed to improve its school system despite a series of reforms in recent years. A more ambitious, national reform strategy is now urgently needed to improve quality and equity in education, according to a new OECD report.

The Swedish education ministers and the head of the National Agency for Education listened to the OECD experts and responded:

> We are welcoming the OECD's report and are now handing it over to the School Commission. The School Commission will, based on among other things the OECD recommendations, present proposals aiming at improved knowledge outcomes, improved quality in education and an increased equivalence in the Swedish school.
>
> (The Swedish Government website 2015)

Some years ago, this would have been regarded as an extraordinary event. Extraordinary not only because the nation-state had long been understood to be sovereign in governing its educational systems, but also because education was considered to be an integrated part of national cultures and specific circumstances that made it more or less unique and incomparable. Given the previously predominant conception of education as being thoroughly intimately formed by cultural and contextual forces in complex interaction (e.g., Kandel 1930), international comparisons by means of school outcomes would have been regarded neither as helpful for improving educational systems (see, e.g., Novoa and Yariv-Mashal 2003) nor as in the national interest. Previously, though international perspectives have been considered interesting to discuss, it would have been regarded as more relevant to take advice from experts that were already in place – a large set of national agencies and institutes whose very mission was to inform and advise the government in educational matters.

Post-political governing 87

There is more to this than the Swedish government simply seeking advice from international experts who, presumably, have not spent much time in Swedish contexts. Rather, we see it as a situation where invited OECD experts are actually setting the agenda, defining the problems in education and presenting suggestions for how to tackle these problems in terms of governance, design of system and curricula. The Swedish government representatives seem to be listening carefully to this expertise and are handing over the OECD recommendations to the Swedish reform commission to consider. Even if educational perspectives have long been welcome in education discourses, we have to ask why such a specific event is possible, what this indicates in terms of politics and educational policy, and, important and not to be forgotten, what this implies for education and for those who are to be educated.

In this chapter, we will deal with this previously strange but now normal way of defining and managing educational policy matters. We will analyse what is special in this kind of 'soft governance', where supranational evidence and recommendations are playing a key role (e.g., Lawn 2006). We will not hesitate to generalise and give a historical view of changes and differences in managing educational systems – their design and content.

The analyses are based on curriculum theory with a Foucauldian twist (e.g., Muller 2012): they place a particular focus on 'the educated' as the key target for education and education policy and as the result of a rather improvised apparatus for the training and fostering of good citizens and reliable persons (Hunter 1994). Analyses of curricula in terms of political socialisation and citizenship education have been carried out by, for example, Englund (1986) and Torney-Purta (2002). Our contribution is carried out with a focus on political subjectivation and education governance. Within the curriculum theory framework outlined above, we take as our point of departure that educational systems and curriculum designs and practises are based on the distinction between the non-educated and the educated as symbols for action and the possibilities to educate. This distinction is basic for capturing educational systems in society (Luhmann and Schorr 2000) within the frameworks or contingencies of particular institutions and histories. From this point of view, educational systems are coded in terms of the educated/non-educated and are central in the processes of fostering individual and political subjectivities. Successes and failures in efforts to make 'the educated' are encoded and embodied in flesh-and-blood individuals. They are framed by constructions of facts and truth regimes concerning the workings of the education system. It is our ambition to present differences in such conceptions in relation to changes in educational policy and governing since WWII in Sweden. We will compare different regulating practises and governing regimes in these respects, and our results will present a set of curriculum codes, each as a summary of who the educated are in terms of political subjectivation – as subjects in political spaces (see, e.g., Simons and Masschelein 2010).

Political projects in education: the politics and the political

Since pre-modern times, education has been a political project and is regarded as essential in the forming of nations, states and citizens. However, it is also a

88   *Rita Foss Lindblad and Sverker Lindblad*

political project that varies over time and contexts and is highly dependent on the ways in which both politics and education have been discursively set and lived. As a consequence, what is to be considered as the political project of education is also a scholarly question that concerns our understandings of politics, education and their interrelatedness.

Thus, our understanding of education as a political project is in need of some clarification. We rely here on what is usually referred to as post-foundational political thought, where the distinction and interrelation between *politics* and *the political* is essential. While politics is a concept referring to the organising and regulative powers of the state and its institutions, the political refers to the ontological dimensions of what are considered to be the targets of politics. Traditionally and in more classical political theories, this ontological dimension has been referred to as an apolitical, primitive and asocial reality in need of political governance, while in recent theories, it refers more to a dynamic force or to a specific domain outside the domain of states and their institutions. This line of thought has been deployed in different ways. For example, in Foucault (1990), the political is seen as present in every human relation organised by power and politics and can be found 'everywhere', while as in Mouffe (2005), it refers to spaces of contingencies, powers and antagonism seen as constitutive of human societies. Despite variances such as these, the relation between politics and the political is seen as highly relative, intimate and without fixed 'ground' or 'foundation' (see Marchart 2007; Szkudlarek 2011).

However, taken outside the realms of political theory and put into the realms of educational theory, our talk about 'the political project of education' must be understood in ways that give specificity to both the political and the educational part of this 'project'. Using the distinction between politics and the political, the political project of education can be said to have two points of reference. It refers, firstly, to the politics of state regulation of education, or what we usually talk about as educational policy and educational governance, and, secondly, to the political as that which is both the target and outcome of this governance. Most significantly, this has concerned the educational constructions and realisations of 'the educated', a social phenomenon mediated and materialised into organisational structures and curricula through different tools and forms of governance and rationales, and categorised as, for example 'population', 'child', 'citizen' or, more recently, 'the life-long learner' (Biesta 2011; Fejes and Dahlstedt 2014; Popkewitz 2014).

Our focus will be on the political and educational constructions of the educated through processes of schooling, policymaking and governance. Seen as an abstraction, 'the educated' become both the target and outcome of political expectations and curricular realisations as well as policies. It refers to a wide range of possibilities for how the very objects and mediums of education have been individuated in categories such as those mentioned above, as well as other categories such as students, teachers, boys, girls etc. Thereby, 'the educated' is understood as a concept having some specific attributes derived in relation to the design of education systems and knowledge organisation summarised as curriculum codes (e.g., Lundgren 1979) and to schooling practises and prospects.

Post-political governing 89

To deal with this as a research problem is basic in curriculum theory, where the perspectives have shifted dependent on how, among many things, the political nature of education has been understood and conceptualised. For example, scholars that rely on what we referred to above as classical political theories might be more likely to address questions such as, 'How, and for whom, is education designed, delivered and assessed?' (see, e.g., Bernstein 2000). Educational scholars relying on more recent political thinking either trace the system of reason embedded within the making of the educated as a heterogeneous and non-essentialist category or more directly address and explore the possibilities of the educated as that 'which is not (yet)' (see, e.g., Biesta 2014; Biesta and Säfström 2011) and which emerges out of the complexity in pedagogical processes in interaction with contexts (Bellman 2013). We will here follow the second line of thought and identify particular and distinct meanings and rationales of what is and is not meant by 'the educated' in different periods of the political and pedagogical making of an educated population in Sweden.

Thus, in the following sections we will analyse key periods in the historical trajectory of the Swedish welfare state educational policy and school governance, from WWII to the present time. Our perspective and overarching aim is, firstly, to identify some distinctive features and embedded meanings of the educated as a target of both schooling and welfare state building within different periods of educational governance, and, secondly, to further explore and discuss these constructs in relation to current neoliberal and post-political governance, as briefly demonstrated in our introduction.

Changing discourses on education and education governance

School governance in the Swedish welfare state has been described as transformed in some distinctive periods of rupture – from, firstly, a centralised system implementing comprehensive school reforms to, secondly, a decentralised system that changed the processes of implementation of the very same reforms (Lindblad and Wallin 1993) and then, thirdly, into a restructured – deregulated and marketised – educational system following a discourse of improved educational efficiency and quality (Lindblad and Lundahl 2001). In the highly globalised system of the 2000s, the governance has, as we intend to show, increasingly come to be based on governing by the politics of numbers and comparisons – between schools, communities, countries and school performers – presenting a seemingly objective and unpolitical view of education and schools. However, the conceptualisation of social phenomena such as these is highly value-loaded and makes a difference in what kinds of educated beings become possible.

We will describe briefly but in some detail these four periods and their political significance. A specific point of interest is to identify and clarify how, and with what means and potential consequences, changes in discourses and governance have a bearing on the making of the educated as a highly elusive and troubling social phenomenon. Each period is summarised in the table below. The summarising curriculum codes are defined and described according to changes in

90 *Rita Foss Lindblad and Sverker Lindblad*

governance, policymaking and relations between such matters, also as state and schooling or teacher-student relations. The presented periods overlap but have their distinctive discursive and political signatures of policymaking, governing and conceptual making of the educated. The point of the periodisation is to use historical variations and emphases in order to clarify differences in educational configurations and curriculum coding considering political subjectivities.

Period 1 – Reformation: Educational policymaking in the first decades after WWII was based on the ambition to educate democratic citizens in a modern welfare state society. The emphasis on democracy was stated as a policymaking response to experiences of totalitarian regimes. Given these experiences, it was felt that education should promote the preservation of democracy and counteract authoritarian tendencies in society. Education as a means to modernise society was to respond to demands for a well-educated population able to deal competently with the demands of that secularisation, rationalisation and industrialisation as well as modes of democracy. During the 1950s, there were extensive political discussions about educational reform, where the policymakers were given legitimacy as elected representatives of the people. Given the demands presented, the outcomes were a comprehensive compulsory school and an integrated upper secondary school. The governing of this modernised education was made by centralised decision-making and standardised solutions to educational problems – often in terms of presenting centrally formulated directives and procedures based on the political authority given by the slogan 'the people for the people'. The educated – codified as the *democratic citizens* – is a social phenomenon of a collective of trained citizens striving for social and economic well-being for themselves as well as for the state.

Period 2 – Decentralisation: The centralised way of governing was increasingly criticised and was transformed by parliamentary decisions into more of a decentralised organisation, based on the belief that the political problems would be best handled by local actors. To formulate this in other terms, education was to be governed from the front (by means of given goals and expectations) and not from behind (by means of centrally formulated directives and procedures). It also implied that there was a need to find ways to realise local governing – for example, by local school boards or boards made up of users of the different schools. In this context, the educated were a social phenomenon mainly codified as *engaged participants* in local matters, also captured as deliberative school democracy, for instance.[1]

Period 3 – Marketisation: However, earlier periods of policymaking and governing were radically challenged and changed by the then-conservative government in the early 1990s, whose major political problem was how to deal with financial unrest and increasing international competition. A neoliberal agenda was introduced in terms of deregulation, privatisation and marketisation and was assumed to govern education in a more efficient and modern way compared to the previous bureaucratic behemoth. Within the discourse, students and parents became consumers in an education 'market', expected to make informed and rational choices in accordance with whatever their future plans were. This in turn presupposed a well-functioning information system providing data on alternatives and their qualities, where school results were regarded as a common denominator. Parallel to this focus on school performance and individual success was the production of a system of basic values considering ethical principles for schooling and upbringing. This transition in discursive positions rewrote the map of the education system (Lindblad and Wallin 1993) and was accompanied by the introduction of New Public Management in schools and communities and led to increased decoupling between different layers in the education system (Lindblad et al. 2002). From this point of view, the educated individual is a versioned persona of one who learns to manage matters of life, here codified as the *informed consumer*, realising the private good of educational offers.

Period 4 – Globalisation: This restructuring changed the structure of actors and conceptions of trust in education. It implied increasing demands for governing by information about measureable school results instead of goals, quality assurance and school inspections, and the government prioritised such issues in the late 1990s (Bergh 2011). Parallel to such measures, information systems comparing schools and communities were developed by the National Agency for Education and introduced in 2000, first as a service only to the local policymakers, but later to be used by mass media and school consumers. A further – and in this context very important – ingredient was the emphasised use of international comparisons of school results such as the OECD Programme for Individual Student Assessment (PISA). Such international measurements were regarded as technical instruments for obtaining evidence concerning the quality of the national education system. This is combined by national and local measurements which put together a system of soft governance in education (see, e.g., Lawn 2006; Sellar and Lingard 2013), where education actors are expected to find ways to improve education outcomes in relation to certain external scales or benchmarks.[2] The educated, as well as education and schooling itself, are here stripped of more complex meanings and instead are reduced and equalised to the results of the measurements – showing different achievement patterns which now becomes the key problem of what should be mastered by the education system as well as the educated. For mastering the role of the educated, the flexible and self-regulating learner with metacognitive skills and abilities to monitor, evaluate and set new agendas for individual improvements becomes the only alternative (see, e.g., Ball 2003, 2012; Dumont et al. 2010).

Table 6.1 summarises these transitions in policymaking and governing over different periods, focusing on differences in expectations concerning the educated. The table presents four ideal types of the educated over periods where variations are emphasised. Thus, there are similarities between the periods and differences within them, but the focus is on what is regarded as the specific and distinct qualities in relation to each period.

There are similar ways of dealing with education politics during the reformation and decentralisation periods – by means of decisions of elected policymakers on national or local levels – but the governing is here understood as radically different. The change from governing from behind by means of centrally decided procedures and directives to governing from the front by means of goals is highly related to the decentralisation of decision-making and a belief in universal educational values; although there are differences in context or local preconditions, there is also a sameness in ambition what is being striven for. In the reformation period, the educated are the democratic citizens following the rules of democratic policymaking in managing the political – by means of government elections – in counteracting authoritarian regimes. In the decentralisation period, the bureaucratic and centralistic management of education has turned into a problem and the educated are characterised as participants in the practises in democratic schooling, for example, in terms of practicing liberal democracy in schools.

A radical break in education politics is presented in the marketisation period, where decentralisation turned into deregulation and the introduction of markets. There are some common ingredients with the decentralised practise in governing from the front, but now in terms of measurements of school performance. The main point concerns changes in policymaking from a system where elected policymakers on different levels make decisions to a system where different stakeholders and actors in the education market are vital ingredients. The market is assumed to regulate education in terms of quality and efficiency by means of informed and rational choices by the customers.

The policymaking and the construction of education markets are assumed to deal with the drawbacks of the expanded welfare state in terms of costs and lack of impact on students and parents in what matters for them in their life and career. Thus, the educated here are the accountable consumers in the so-called education market, where the object is to maximise the private good by means of accountable choices from education alternatives. An important aspect of this marketisation is the need for transparent and trustworthy production of information for different stakeholders, for the state, for the competing providers of educational alternatives and for the customers. For instance, information on school performance in governing by results is instrumental in relation to the functioning of the market.

This focus on school performance is further exaggerated in the globalisation period, where the qualities of education performance are measured at a global level and where international agents are at work in providing information on these qualities by means of international comparisons and assessments by international

Table 6.1 The educated in curriculum codes in different periods of policymaking and governing in Sweden 1945–2015.[3]

Period	Policymaking	Emphasis in governing	The educated as curriculum code
Reformation	Parliamentary reform decisions	Governing from behind	Democratic citizen
Decentralisation	Local community and school users	Governing from the front	Engaged participant
Marketisation	Market acting and consumer choice	Governing by markets	Informed and rational customer
Globalisation	Framed by international expertise	Soft governance	Self-regulating performer

experts. Here, such performance and advice are constructing a truth regime working in a global arena framing the agenda of the local actors (see, e.g., Bauman 1998). This regime is changing the position of the government, as stated at the beginning of this text. But it is also reframing the educated into tested performers serving as informants in a self-regulating education system, where comparisons of school results matter most in the hunt for the effective school. Education is subsumed under test results, and educational interventions are regarded as instrumental in relation to school performance.

To end this section: the ideal types presented here have to be understood as constellations that are overlapping in time and context, but are also *marked by different rationalities*. For instance, the marketisation of education is very much present in the globalisation period, but the latter must be regarded as an intensification and translation of the importance of school performance and international competition. Here, school performances come to be regarded not only as measured outcomes of the efficiency and quality of educational systems, but translated into the very essence of education, to what it is all about. When subsumed under such a rationality, educational policy and governance become instrumental and dependent on indicator systems and external evaluations, and what is lost, or invisible, is the myriad of impulses, possibilities and actual problematics that are inscribed in educational activities and their forming of political subjectivities. To our understanding, this also means that the important political ambition of education to allow for new, alternative forms of beings is neglected, which actually means that they are denied as political targets within current educational endeavours.

The OECD at work in educational settings

Let us now go more specifically into the event that we outlined in the introduction. Here, we could note an interaction between different actors: the Swedish government, the OECD, the research program PISA, mass-media reporters and so forth. More precisely, three aspects are put forward in the OECD experts' view on Swedish education: declining school quality, increased differences between schools and increasing segregation in terms of differences between students with different socio-economic backgrounds.

The education problematics outlined by the experts are as follows:

> Education is a public priority in Sweden. However, over the past decade, average performance in Sweden declined from a level above or around the OECD average to below the average in all three core subjects (reading, mathematics and science) measured in the Programme for International Student Assessment (PISA) (OECD 2015). Though other international data sources and national data had previously shown there was reason to be concerned about the quality of the school system, the disappointing performance on PISA 2012 further sparked the national debate on quality and equity and the future of education in Sweden. This resulted in a broad consensus among educators and politicians on the need for change.
>
> (OECD 2015, p. 14)

The PISA results, as measured by individual student performances, are treated as solid facts by the OECD experts. But the facts also become key actors in this scenario and seem to require specific actions in order to counteract the current declining status of education in Sweden. More precisely, the basis for the statements is not only derived from empirical evidence from performances of a sample of Swedish students on standardised achievement tests on 'core subjects' (mathematics, reading and science), but the tests themselves are believed to measure competencies at a level that is important for 'participating in life'. The OECD experts state, for instance, that Swedish students are below average in mathematics performance, but somewhat above average in terms of socio-economic equity in these performances. However, to these statements, the experts add that test performance is constantly declining over a longer period of time and so is equity, as measured by the increasing impact of student socio-economic background on test performance.[4] Given these developments, the OECD (2015, p.3) makes recommendations and '. . . identifies three priorities for Sweden, namely to:

- Establish the conditions that promote quality with equity across Swedish schools.
- Build capacity for teaching and learning through a long-term human resource strategy.
- Strengthen the steering of policy and accountability with a focus on improvement'.

To this the experts add: 'The OECD is there to help Sweden rise to that challenge' (OECD 2015, p. 3). Thus, the OECD's work combines a specific way of defining educational problems with hopes to manage these problems and to improve the quality of education in Sweden – in some specific but not openly declared ways. What is not declared is that the facts get their meanings and become actionable only within a specific discourse on what education and the educated are and are expected to be. Below, we will analyse the premises for making such statements by, firstly, looking more carefully at the evidence put forward and, secondly, looking at the political as well as educational specificity of the situation.

Analysing premises of OECD evidence as a style of reasoning

The OECD evidence is based on a specific way of obtaining knowledge about education. Here we turn to Hacking (1992a) (see also Lindblad et al. 2015), who analyses different styles of reasoning in the history of science (e.g., analogue models, experiments and observations). This is an alternative to the Kuhn (1962) approach to capturing scientific paradigms and based on the work of Crombie (1994) on the history of science. Premises and implications of such styles of reasoning are important to capture in order to understand the epistemic and ontological foundations for what counts as evidence and standards for objectivity and demarcations between truth and falsehood. Thus, identifying styles of reasoning can improve our understanding of the constraints and opportunities of different ways of gaining and producing knowledge.

Post-political governing   95

The research presented by the OECD uses a style of 'statistical analysis' dealing with patterns of relations between variables and categories and based on decontextualisation and universalistic knowledge interests. This style was developed during the nineteenth and early twentieth centuries, marked by, for example, the emergence of probability, the theory of error and the creation of statistical objects (Hacking 1992b, p. 141 f.). Such developments served as preconditions for presenting and evaluating statements on the education of a population (Lindblad et al. 2015, p. 19):

- by ways of defining and analysing populations (comparing, for instance, countries or educational systems) and their characteristics
- by formulating procedures or methods for the production of valid statements, such as demands on strength of association or significance tests
- by measuring means and variations in performances by means of certain tests
- by developing taxonomic groups (in terms of socio-economic indicators, sex or cultures) and comparing their progress and failures in educational matters

PISA is an international research program that is characterised by such a style of reasoning. It is a program based on large-scale assessment and standardised achievement tests carried out in different contexts. As such, it has several validity problems – for example, when doing comparisons over different contexts (see, e.g., Berliner 2015) – but we will focus here on implications of the statistical style of reasoning in education policymaking and the construct of the educated.

The facts produced by PISA cannot be understood as facts about education or educational performance in a 'real' sense (if 'real' here supposes a correspondence between factual statements and the concrete objects they refer to). Instead, PISA research analyses patterns and associations between variables in large databases (e.g., in terms of ranking of performances by country, which seems to be important in the OECD definition of problems with education in Sweden) or between student interest (e.g., in science) and performance in science achievement tests. These are correlations, not to be confused with explanations in terms of causal mechanisms. Stated otherwise, this is a vital constraint that must be considered in statistical reasoning.

Furthermore, research such as in the PISA studies is able to produce correlations and differences – for example, categorising people or populations into different kinds – but has little to say about causes and effects from the findings produced. For instance, in PISA studies, there are a number of analyses in terms of achievement gaps between categories put into taxonomic groups, where individuals in one category are assumed to share similar properties and to be different from other categories, such as between 'socio-economically disadvantaged and advantaged individuals', 'boys and girls' or between 'immigrants or non-immigrants', for instance, as presented in the Sweden report:

> Students with immigrant background scored 58 points less in mathematics performance in PISA 2012. This is among the largest differences in OECD countries (average difference of 34 points), but a decrease compared to the

96 *Rita Foss Lindblad and Sverker Lindblad*

difference in Sweden between mathematics performance of non-immigrant and immigrant students in PISA 2003 (64 points).

(OECD 2015, p. 81)

However, as large-scale studies and statistical analyses such as those produced and used here have the advantage of being replicable in new measurements, they also have the disadvantage of limited explanatory powers (in contrast to, for example, intensive studies such as case studies, where it is possible to identify causes or to explain certain events in context (see Sayer 2000; von Wright 1983). As it seems, the very use and political implications drawn from these studies seem to be contrary to their epistemological and methodological characteristics (of limitations as well as advantages). When and if, for example, the studied results of tests become equalised or read as facts applicable to actual individuals (instead of the studies' abstract categories), the risk of stigmatisation as well as the reproduction of prejudices would be high.

Expanding statistical evidence into educational recommendations

This way of analysing educational matters by means of large-scale assessments makes it possible to produce overviews and identify problems within educational systems on a descriptive and representative level of generalisation. However, what we witness is that such studies have also been used for purposes of practical guidance, which is problematic, to say the least. And despite the fact that there are researchers within the field who *deny* that they are identifying causalities and causal mechanisms (see, e.g., Woessmann 2011, who emphasises this limit), others make such claims and don't hesitate to put forward recommendations based on their findings, saying for example:

> . . . 55% of students report that their teachers practise similar tasks until they know that students have understood the task (OECD average 67%). Also, less than 49% of Swedish teachers refer to situations from everyday life or work to demonstrate why a problem is important (OECD average 68%) (OECD 2015). Evidence points towards the effectiveness of connecting learning with real-world situations rather than learning abstract concepts without seeing their practical application.
>
> (Guthrie et al. 2012) (OECD 2015, p. 77)

But if the priorities stated in the OECD report regarding what political actions should be taken into account in matters of educational policy do not follow from the evidence given by the PISA research, it should follow that the OECD experts are operating far beyond the rules of statistical reasoning. One conclusion is that a specific type of scientific reasoning has become not only politically used, but also politically inscribed and made into an effective tool for educational governing within *some* specific contexts.

This particular way of governing and 'policing' education is problematic. What we are witnessing is a matter of transformations within educational systems and welfare states where a performance-based 'truth regime' (see Krejsler et al. 2014) has come to dominate the organisation of education. Thus, what we are up against is regulation and governance with some specific political and epistemic significance regarding what education, teachers and pupils/students are, and how their futures ought to be organised. It is also true, however, that the normative and universal claims made present an effective obstacle to alternatives.

What was the case, then? Concluding remarks on curriculum codes and political subjectivation

Seen solely in terms of educational governance, the 'odd' and extraordinary type of educational governance demonstrated in our introduction by the interaction between OECD experts and the Swedish government may not appear odd at all. It may simply be seen as different, as just another regime of governance with differences from and similarities to other such regimes. Even though this conclusion makes sense, it makes sense only if we deny ourselves the opportunity to reflect about what is 'not so evident' when it comes to education and educational policy. While, for example, it is evident that both education and educational policy change over time, and that the changes themselves have something to do with changes in society as well as politics, the political nature of the theoretical frameworks that frame such thinking and acting are often forgotten or neutralised.

It has been our ambition to highlight such politics, where in this text the 'not so evident' about the interacting of education, education policy and thinking has turned into a concern about the educated. 'The educated' is here understood at once as the target and outcome of education as well as of educational policy, and as referring to a wide range of *possibilities* of educational organisations, offers and subjectivities allowed for within the realms of 'the educated'. It is, we will claim, also with regard to the educated that the present regime of governance seems grave in its consequences.

When education and the educated as social phenomena are normatively turned into statistical universals, we are not only confronted with reductionism of a sort that makes us wish for more robust understandings and explanations. Even more seriously, these seemingly neutral and unmarked figures are highly political as well as performative and very effective at hiding the political character of education as well as the educated as emergent phenomena (Bellmann 2013) – and therefore also effective at hindering the making of alternative educational and political subjectivities. The curriculum code of a self-regulative performer acting within the frames of soft governance and international assessment is a signifier of an instrumental and technified education system of governmental subjectivation (Simons and Masschelein 2010) that very much needs to be analysed and compared to other ways of curriculum design and education governance with other kinds of political subjectivation. However, and what must be remembered as most important, the possibilities of education to transform into a more democratic endeavour are highly dependent on our capacity to think and act outside of the box of the 'present as well as the past' (as we know and identify it also in terms of politics and democracy). This, among

98 *Rita Foss Lindblad and Sverker Lindblad*

many things, requires that we address also the possibilities of what could come true in terms of possibilities and potential beings.

Notes

1   This ideal type is constructed as a combination of the educated individual as a democratic citizen and a participant in dealing with local matters. A way to conceptualise this is in terms of deliberative democracy (e.g., Englund 1986; Habermas 1984).
2   Notions of soft governance and an open method of coordination are important in current transnational as well as national and local governance. For instance, Ozga (2009) states that 'traditional forms of education government through rule-governed processes, centralised legal frameworks and shared assumptions . . . in place from the 1870s to the 1970s, were replaced in the late twentieth and early twenty-first century by goal-governed steering of outputs and outcomes, accompanied by the monitoring of targets. In soft governance evaluation and self-regulation play important parts, but . . . the local and the local authority appear to have lost their position and their place' (p. 160). Thus, soft governance does not mean that central authorities have loosened their command on education.
    The open method rests on soft-law mechanisms such as guidelines and indicators, benchmarking and sharing of best practises. This means that there are no official sanctions for laggards. Rather, the method's effectiveness relies on a form of peer pressure and naming and shaming, as no member state wants to be seen as the worst in a given policy area.
3   In Table 6.1, we are emphasising differences between periods. In the table, it is important to recognise that there is a continuity over periods; for example, parliamentary decision-making also matters in the post-political period, which also has several elements in common with the restructuring period.
4   *Improving Schools in Sweden: An OECD perspective.* OECD 2015, p. 32.

References

Ball, S.J. (2003). The teacher's soul and the terrors of performativity. *Journal of Education Policy* 18(2): 215–228.
Ball, S.J. (2012). Performativity, commodification and commitment: An I-Spy guide to the neoliberal university. *British Journal of Educational Studies* 60(1): 17–28.
Bauman, Z. (1998). *Globalization.* Cambridge: Polity.
Bellmann, J. (2013). The changing field of educational studies and the task of theorizing education. In G. Biesta, J. Allan and R. Edwards (Eds.), *Making a difference in theory: The theory question in education and the education question in theory* (pp. 65–81). New York: Routledge.
Bergh, A. (2011). Why quality in education–and what quality?–A linguistic analysis of the concept of quality in Swedish government texts. *Education Inquiry* 2(4): 709–723.
Berliner, D. (2015). The implications of understanding that PISA is simply another standardized achievement test. Paper presented at the Numbers Symposium in Gothenburg, June 2015.
Bernstein, B. (2000). *Pedagogy, symbolic control & identity: Theory, research & critique.* London: Taylor & Francis.
Biesta, G. (2011). The ignorant citizen: Mouffe, Rancière, and the subject of democratic education. *Studies in Philosophy and Education* 30: 141–153.

Biesta, G. and Säfström, C.A. (2011). A manifesto for education. *Policy Futures in Education* 9(5): 540–547.

Biesta, G. (2014a). *The beautiful risk of education*. London: Paradigm Publishers.

Crombie, A.C. (1994). *Styles of scientific thinking in the European tradition: The history of argument and explanation especially in the mathematical and biomedical sciences and arts* (Vol. 3). London: Duckworth.

Dumont, H., Instance, D. and Benavides, F. (2010). Analysing and designing learning environments for the 21st century. In H. Humont, D. Instance and F. Benavides (Eds.), *The nature of learning: Using research to inspire practice* (pp. 19–33). Paris: OECD Publishing.

Englund, T. (1986). Curriculum as a political problem. Changing educational conceptions, with special reference to citizenship education. *Uppsala Studies in Education 25*. Lund: Studentlitteratur/Chartwell Bratt.

Fejes, A. and Dahlstedt, M. (2014). The confessing society: Foucault, confession and practices of lifelong learning. Abingdon, Oxon, & New York: Routledge.

Foucault, M. (1990). *The care of the self*. London: Penguin Books.

Guthrie, John T., Allan Wigfield, and Susan Lutz Klauda. (2012). "Adolescents' engagement in academic literacy." *Adolescents' engagement in academic literacy*. Sharjah: UAE: Bentham Science Publishers.

Habermas, J. (1984). *The theory of communicative action* (Vol. I). Boston: Beacon.

Hacking, I. (1992a) "Style" for historians and philosophers. *Studies in the History and Philosophy of Science* 23(1): 1–20.

Hacking, I. (1992b). Statistical language, statistical truth, and statistical reason: The self-authentication of a style of scientific reasoning. In E. McMullin (Ed.), *Social dimensions of science* (pp. 130–157). Notre Dame, IN: University of Notre Dame Press.

Hunter, I. (1994). *Rethinking the school: Subjectivity, bureaucracy, criticism*. St. Leonards: Allen & Unwin Pty Ltd.

Kandel, I.L. (1930). *Essays in comparative education* (pp. 92–94). New York: Teachers College, Columbia University.

Krejsler, J.B., Olsson, U. and Petersson, K. (2014). The transnational grip on Scandinavian education reforms: The open method of coordination challenging national policy-making. *Nordic Studies in Education* 34(3): 172–186.

Kuhn, T.S. (1962). *The structure of scientific revolutions*. Chicago: University of Chicago Press.

Lawn, M. (2006). Soft governance and the learning spaces of Europe. *Comparative European Politics* 4(2–3): 272–288.

Lindblad, S. and Lundahl, L. (2001). Från medborgare till systemoperatör? (From Citizens to System Operator?). In Agell, A. (Red.), *Fostrar skolan goda medborgare?*(pp. 183–210). Uppsala: IUSTUS FÖRLAG AB.

Lindblad, S., Lundahl, L., Lindgren, J. and Zackari, G. (2002). Educating for the New Sweden? *Scandinavian Journal of Educational Research* 46(3): 283–303.

Lindblad, S., Pettersson, K. and Popkewitz, T.S. (2015). *A systematic research review on international comparisons of school performances*. Stockholm: Vetenskapsrådet.

Lindblad, S. and Wallin, E. (1993). On transitions of power, democracy and education in Sweden. *Journal of Curriculum Studies* 25(1): 77–88.

Luhmann, N. and Schorr, K. (2000). *Problems of reflection in the system of education*. Münster: Waxmann.

Lundgren, U.P. (Ed.) (1979). *Code, context and curriculum processes*. Malmö: CWK Gleerup.

100 *Rita Foss Lindblad and Sverker Lindblad*

Marchant, O. (2007). *Post-foundational political thought: Political difference in Nancy, Lefort, Badiou and Laclau*. Edinburgh: Edinburgh University Press.

Mouffe, C. (2005). *The return of the political* (Vol. 8). London & New York: Verso.

Muller, J. (2012). Reclaiming knowledge: Social theory, curriculum and education policy. London: Routledge.

Nóvoa, A. and Yariv-Mashal, T. (2003) Comparative research in education: A mode of governance or a historical journey? *Comparative Education* 39(4): 423–438.

OECD (2015). *Improving schools in Sweden: An OECD perspective*. Available at: http://www.oecd.org/edu/school/Improving-Schools-in-Sweden.pdf

Ozga, J. (2009). Governing education through data in England: From regulation to self-evaluation. *Journal of Education Policy* 24(2): 149–162.

Popkewitz, T. (2014). The empirical and political 'fact' of theory in the social and education sciences. In G. Biesta, J. Allen and R. Edwards (Eds.), *Making a difference in theory: The theory question in education and the education question in theory* (pp. 13–29). New York: Routledge.

Sayer, A. (2000). *Method in social science: A realist approach*. London and New York: Routledge.

Sellar, S. and Lingard, B. (2013). The OECD and global governance in education. *Journal of Education Policy* 28(5): 710–725.

Simons, M. and Masschelein, J. (2010). Governmental, political and pedagogic subjectivation: Foucault with Rancière. *Educational Philosophy and Theory* 42(5–6): 588–605.

The Swedish Government website. (2015). Available at: http://www.regeringen.se/pressmeddelanden/2015/05/oecd-overlamnar-granskning-av-svensk-skola/

Szkudlarek, T. (2011). Semiotics of identity: Politics and education. *Studies in Philosophy and education* 30(2): 113–125.

Torney-Purta, J. (2002). The school's role in developing civic engagement: A study of adolescents in twenty-eight countries. *Applied Developmental Science* 6(4): 203–212.

Woessmann, L. (2011). Cross-country evidence on teacher performance pay. *Economics of Education Review* 30(3): 404–418.

von Wright, G.H. (1983). *Practical Reason*. Oxford: Blackwell.

7 Why education? Economic and political subjectivities in public discourses on education[1]

Eva Reimers

> Projections based on historical relationships (bearing in mind the uncertainties of future projections) suggest that if all OECD countries could boost their average PISA scores by 25 points over the next two decades, the aggregate gain of OECD GDP would be USD 115 trillion over the lifetime of the generation born in 2010 . . . Bringing all countries up to the OECD's best performing education system in PISA, Finland, would result in gains in the order of USD 260 trillion. It is the quality of learning outcomes, not the length of schooling, which makes the difference.
>
> (OECD 2012b, p. 90)

> Efficient investment in human capital through education and training systems is an essential component of Europe's strategy to deliver the high levels of sustainable, knowledge-based growth and jobs that lie at the heart of the Lisbon strategy, at the same time as promoting personal fulfilment, social cohesion and active citizenship.
>
> (European Union 2009, p. 1)

> A quality education throughout life is the birthright of every woman, man and child. In turn, education, particularly that of girls and women, aids progress across all development goals.
>
> (UNESCO 2011, p. 5)

The quotations above give different answers to the question of why education is important. The OECD (OECD 2012b) publication as well as the EU (2009) publication are both expressive of education as an economic investment leading to economic gains, even if the latter also points to education as a means to reach social cohesion and personal fulfilment. The UNESCO (2011) publication is instead expressive of education as a human right.

In this chapter, I will scrutinise some documents from the OECD, the EU and UNESCO in order to discuss and ask questions about how the entanglements of economic, social and educational norms make way for and preclude the emergence of political subjectivity. I therefore use the question 'Why education?' in order to map how intersections of norms and discourses produce different notions of why nations, organisations and individuals should spend time and money on education.

102 *Eva Reimers*

The introductory quotations give different answers to the questions of why education is important and why nations should therefore spend money and effort on education. It is notable that, from an area that has been regarded as a predominantly national concern, education has in the recent decades more and more become a concern for multilateral organisations, and they, as exemplified by the quotations above, have specific interests with respect to how and why nations should pursue education. The quotations all point to education as a prerequisite for a good future. But good for whom, and good in what way? In the quotations, the outcomes of education are described with words such as 'gains', 'fulfilment' and 'progress', constructing the goals for the future in economic terms. They also demonstrate that the gains of education can be constructed slightly differently. They point in different directions. The first quotation points to education as a means to foster economic growth and progress. The OECD report *Education at a Glance* (OECD 2012a), which is a summary of the results of the Programme for International Student Assessment (PISA) tests, uses specific amounts of USD to describe the value and gains of educational achievements. The value of education is here expressed in strictly economic terms. In a similar way, the EU document *Education and Training 2020* (European Union 2009) uses the wording 'invest in human capital' in referring to education and training in the member states. The gains of these investments, however, are described in less monetary terms than in the OECD document. Instead of solely leading to economic gains, in the EU document they are expressed as being in the interest of society as well as in the interest of the individual. For society, education will produce 'social cohesion' and active citizens, whereas education will lead to 'personal fulfilment' for the individual. The economic gain is present in the quotation in terms of the vaguer expression 'knowledge-based growth'. The UNESCO document *UNESCO and Education* (UNESCO 2011) shows a slightly different take on why education is important by referring to education as a 'birthright', that is, presenting education as a human right. However, this is not the sole motivation. The second sentence says that education 'aids progress across all development goals'. So even if education on the one hand is constructed as a human right for individuals, it is simultaneously made into an asset for everybody. Together, the quotations point to education as a means to foster economic growth and progress, but also as a human right that increases opportunities for the learning subjects. But what about political subjectivity? What about education as a space where subjects can emerge who can and want to partake in forming a more democratic, just and equal world? The EU quotation uses the terms 'social cohesion' and 'active citizenship' as positive democratic outcomes of education. Maybe this could open up for political subjectivity as a goal for educational endeavours.

Impact, governance and assemblage

One point of departure for the chapter is the notion of education as a widespread discursive and material assemblage, with no definite or clear boundaries in either content or space. Discourses, practises, norms, money, ideology and people are continuously entangled in different ways, constituting differing educational normative materialities. Education takes place in educational institutions, in everyday life and on the Internet. It can be formal, informal, intentional or unintentional. One example of the messiness of education is that although comprehensive education is often considered a national concern and a national project, the assemblage of education is by no means limited to the borders of the nation states (cf. Foss Lindblad and Lindblad, Chapter 6 in this book). Transnational and multilateral interests, companies and agents invest money, time and effort into what in many ways can be described as an international educational market with an ensuing denationalisation of education (cf. Ball 2012). Another aspect of the denationalisation of education is the multilateral organisations (e.g., organisations concerned with economic or political cooperation and/or cooperation on issues of peace and human rights) that have demonstrated an interest in the field of education and have directed funds to that end. Their entanglement in the education practises of nations is not only a matter of showing an interest in education. As shown by, for example, Rita Foss Lindblad and Sverker Lindblad in this book, they play an active role in governing education. The most evident example of multilateral influence and governance of education worldwide is the OECD's PISA, which has expanded the field of comparative education in an unprecedented way (Meyer and Benavot 2013). Through PISA, the OECD has taken on the role not only of diagnostician but also of policy advisor for national school systems. As Heinz-Dieter Meyer and Aaron Benavot assert, this has created a situation where state sovereignty over education is replaced by multilateral organisations, and 'the very meaning of public education is being recast from a project aimed at forming national citizens and nurturing social solidarity to a project driven by economic demands and labour market orientation' (Meyer and Benavot 2013, p. 10). In this way, denationalisation is combined with economic colonisation. The notion of education as subsumed by the demands of the economy can by and large be understood as an outcome of the hegemony of neoliberal economic norms, which makes economic growth into the overriding engine and goal for society. The interests of the economic market (of capitalism) are made tantamount to the interests of nations.

Considering the impact of multilateral organisations on policies, public discourses and research, it is important to critically explore how these organisations conceive of education, and what this makes way for. The education research community has produced a considerable amount of critical research, especially concerning the international comparative studies of student achievement such as Trends in International Mathematics and Science Study (TIMSS) and PISA. The reports of these studies have thus instigated what can almost be described as a new research field of 'critical PISA studies'. There are studies of how different countries have responded to their own results in terms of 'PISA shock' (Gruber 2006; Pons 2012; Takayama 2008). There are studies that are critical of the contextual insensitivity in conducting large-scale cross-national comparative tests related to learning outcomes (Kamens 2013; Sjöberg 2015). Others question the validity of comparing results from different years, based on the insight that the population of students can never be the same from year to year (Berliner 2015). There is also criticism about how PISA neglects and obfuscates the most apparent

104 Eva Reimers

factor for school success, that is, social and economic background, with critics claiming that the tests are actually much more reflective of sociological variables than they are of educational variables (Condor 2011). Another point of critique concerns the way in which the student achievement surveys have become tools for governance of education (Ball 2013; Grek 2009; Grek et.al. 2015). Following from this, there is also research that focuses on how the international tests have instigated national standardised and high-stakes testing, turning education into 'teaching for the test'; successful test results have thereby come to be used as the most evident goal for teachers, influencing what should be taught and how (Biesta 2010).

Taken together, the multitude of critical PISA studies evince how the multilateral governance of education in the form of comparative tests, the reports of these tests and the recommendations that follow contribute to a construction of a notion of education limited to what can be assessed and measured in achievement tests on science, mathematics and literacy. More general and more major objectives of comprehensive education, such as supporting democratic values, creating equality and forming a desired community and sense of citizenship, are not measured and thereby not included in what is considered quality of education. This is also the case for subjects such as the arts, physical education, history and social science. They are devalued by being excluded from international achievement tests. If we believe that education can and should be a space for the emergence of political subjectivity, the narrow view of education in the global education discourse might be an obstacle. It is therefore critical to ask questions about what subjectivities are made possible or emerge from how education is constructed in the documents on education from multilateral organisations. Like Foss Lindblad and Lindblad in Chapter 6, I therefore ask: what and who are the educated expected to become in the documents? What form of agency are they expected to enact, and what is their role in an imagined future presumed to be?

The introductory quotations above evince simultaneous dissimilar normative materialisations of different norms in relation to education (cf. Chan 2007). One important presumption for this chapter is that the salience of differing discursive frames and rationalities in the multilateral public education discourse has consequences for how to make sense of education in both a global and local perspective. Differing ideas about how education is to be conceived, how it should be practised, who it is for and what the content and the expected outcome should be connect, or plug into, differing assemblages or discourses constructing not only education, but also economy, politics, nationhood, citizenship, work, development, the future etc. As stated in chapter eight of this book, those of us who are positioned in what can be labelled a privileged place are presently in a situation that calls for political subjectivity. There is consequently a need for people who realise that things are bad, that things could be not only different but better and that they themselves are agents in changing things for the better. Refugees seeking refuge from war and poverty; global warming; the increasing influence of racist and nationalist movements; terrorism; and a growing acceptance of intolerance, xenophobia, sexism and Islamophobia can easily give the impression that the present situation isn't good. This is the first step in political subjectivity.

Why education? 105

A question for this chapter is therefore whether and how the conceptions of education constructed in documents by multilateral organisations facilitate the emergence of the notion that something is wrong, and even more important, whether and how they contribute to the emergence of visions that things could be different and that the educated individual her/himself could be an agent in forming a desired future signified by the democratic values of freedom, equality and interdependence. I therefore ask questions concerning the possible subjectivities that emerge from how the organisations formulate objectives, aims and means in the field of education.

Perspectives and theoretical framework

The chapter draws on post-structural perspectives on texts and discourses (Laclau and Mouffe 1985). The post-structural perspective points to a non-foundational and non-intentional approach. Consequently, the texts are not regarded as reflections of ideologies or specific aims. The focus is therefore not on identifying intentions or objectives, but on investigating conceptions and subjectivities emerging from the text. This is further emphasised by viewing the texts from a post-humanist perspective, which shifts the focus from regarding texts as human products to an approach where they are seen as productive materialities (Barad 2007; Deleuze and Guattari 1988), that is, a shift of interest from how they have been made and what their intentions are to what they make way for. Drawing on Gilles Deleuze and Félix Guattari (1988), I conceive of the texts as assemblages where elements such as politicians, policymakers, business interests, comparative assessment surveys, economy, educational practises, administrators, teachers and students, values, desires and aspirations plug into each other forming molar lines, that is, stabilisations of institutionalised desires, as well as lines of flight, that is, deterritorialisations opening up for the unexpected and new.

I find that combining post-structuralist discourse theory and the post-human Deleuzian theoretical toolkit and concepts makes it possible to 'map' intersections, connections and 'pluggings' of different practises, articulations and/or materialisations as open and undecided assemblages, and to explore how these assemblages make possible and obfuscate differing possibilities in terms of the aims of education and subject positions of those who are to be educated. In investigating constitutions of subjectivity in discourses on education, I am also indebted to Gert Biesta's analytical concepts of education as encompassing qualification, socialisation and subjectification (Biesta 2010; 2014a). These are useful concepts in the analysis of how education is constituted and what these constitutions entail in relation to knowledge and subjectivity. The chapter is based on a notion of education as on the one hand practises and on the other hand politics. It is the latter that makes me ask questions about what subjectivities emerge from the notion of education that is constituted in the texts.

Education in EU, OECD and UNICEF documents

The EU, the OECD and UNESCO produce an immense quantity of documents and web pages on education.[2] Considering that education has historically been

106 Eva Reimers

regarded as a national task and endeavour, this is conspicuous. The way in which these multilateral organisations intervene in domestic affairs can on the one hand be seen as a subversion of the notion of independent nation states. On the other hand, by drawing on results and targets from the organisations, the nation states present themselves as attentive to international demands and use these results to present themselves as successful in relation to those who appear less successful. In this way, the cohesion and stability of the imagined nation are stabilised.

The EU and education

The cooperation in the EU has two main and intertwined objectives. One is economic cooperation to ensure continuous economic growth, and the other is political cooperation to secure peace in Europe. The EU forms common educational policies for Europe, influences national educational reforms and also funds educational projects within and outside the EU. The reason the EU produces documents intervening in education is that the organisation wants to make Europe 'more compatible on a global market' (European Union 2009). EU educational initiatives have been – and are – influential in instigating policy changes. One example is the mainstreaming of European higher education in the Bologna Process.

OECD and education

The objective of the OECD is 'to promote policies that will improve the economic and social well-being of people around the world' (OECD 2012a). The OECD is influential in the global educational arena, not least because of PISA, which was launched and is monitored by the OECD. Like the EU, the OECD is not primarily an expert organisation on education. Its main objective is to sustain economic growth (Bank 2012). Since PISA was launched in 2000, the OECD has become a policy actor with global authority. As is well known, PISA is repeatedly referred to by policymakers and in media representations of education in different countries. The outcomes of this global ranking are given considerable attention in public discourses. Furthermore, besides PISA, rankings from the International Association for the Evaluation of Educational Achievement (TIMMS) and the Progress in International Reading Literacy Study instigate and are used in arguments for educational reforms.

UNESCO and education

Differing from the EU and the OECD, which are both organisations for economic cooperation, the mission of UNESCO '. . . is to contribute to the building of peace, the eradication of poverty, sustainable development and intercultural dialogue through education, the sciences, culture, communication and information' (UNESCO 2013a). UNESCO is important in the global educational arena, publishing global reports on education and running educational projects in different parts of the world in cooperation not only with governments, but also with

NGOs and companies. Like the EU and the OECD, UNESCO is an influential agent in global education, not least in the developing countries.

Reading the documents

In order to explore relations between constitutions of education and possibilities for emergence of political subjectivity, I have chosen to analyse documents where the organisations present their work and their aims. From the EU, I have chosen the document *Education and Training 2020* – ET2020 – (European Union 2009), where the commission presents its educational strategy to make the EU into 'a world-leading knowledge economy' (European Union 2009, p. 2). The OECD documents I use for this chapter are the report '*Education at a Glance 2012*' (OECD 2012a) and the OECD report on education '*Education Today 2013*' (OECD 2012b). Concerning UNESCO, I have looked at the web page for the directorate of education (UNESCO 2013a) and the brochure presenting the work and goals of the directorate (UNESCO 2011). I regard these different multilateral documents as interventions plugging into educational politics and policies.

The discussion is based on reading the multilateral documents on education together, reading them through each other and through some of the theoretical concepts of Deleuze and Guattari (1988), as well as the concept of political subjectivity, a concept indebted to Biesta's concept of political (democratic) subjectification (Biesta 2014b). The ambition has been to map similar 'plugging ins' in the different documents in the form of intertextual articulations, that is, articulations repeated and reiterated within and between the texts, but also to map plugging ins of education with other norms that appear specific to the documents. My interest is in investigating how these (de/re)territorialisations of norms concerning education constitute differing concepts of what education is and can accomplish. In this way, I can explore what possible economic and political subject positions emerge from the documents. The focus is thus on the documents as productive, rather than as products.

Education and/as economy

Reiterations and reterritorialisations of concepts and ideas

In reading the documents from the three organisations together, it becomes evident that they belong to the same education assemblage, an assemblage where education is intertwined with, or plugged into, economy as well as equity and citizenship. Similarities between the documents are by no means surprising. There is a considerable overlapping of the constituencies of these organisations. Most EU member states are also members of the OECD and UNESCO. Furthermore, they have a history of cooperation on educational matters, not least between the EU and the OECD. In addition, there is a movement of staff between the organisations (Schuetze 2006, p. 296), and UNESCO receives funding from the OECD and the EU in order to participate in international assessment studies (Kamens 2013).

108 *Eva Reimers*

There are, consequently, apparent similarities between how the objectives of education are constructed in the documents. As is evident from the introductory quotations, one similarity is how they all constitute education as a tool for prosperity and a better future. This is especially evident in *Education at a Glance* (OECD 2012a), where the bulk of the text deals with education in terms of investments and returns, not with the content of education or educational goals. Also, the terminology of strategic or overarching goals is strikingly similar. The EU's strategic objectives of 'lifelong learning', 'improving quality and efficiency', 'promoting equity, social cohesion and active citizenship' and 'enhancing creativity and innovation' (European Union 2009, p. 3) are repeated in the OECD and UNESCO documents with identical or similar wordings (see, e.g., OECD 2012a, p. 13). Furthermore, all three organisations stress the need for lifelong learning as a process that begins with early childhood education and continues through the whole life course, thereby constituting education as a never-ending project. Another similarity is that they take for granted that education should be (and thereby construct it as) something that should be arranged, monitored and financed by public means by the governments in the different countries. Hence, they assert compulsory education as a public good. UNESCO states that their mission is to 'help countries to develop inclusive, holistic and balanced education systems from early childhood to the adult years' (UNESCO 2011, p. 16). Although UNESCO recounts cooperation with NGOs and the private sector (UNESCO 2013b), the responsibility for education is attributed to nation states. This is also the case for the OECD (OECD 2012b, pp. 11–13) and the EU, which asks 'member states' to adhere to a common framework for 'national education' (European Union 2009). A common global and transnational discourse of education emerges from reading the documents, signified by entanglements of education and economy, as well as notions of citizenship and the need for everybody to be subjected to unceasing education. People are thus constituted as always becoming in the interest of the global community, the economy and the nation states.

Education as investment and/or human right

But there are also differences. There is a contrast between the OECD documents and the EU documents on the one hand and the UNESCO documents on the other (cf. Schuetze 2006, p. 295). The aim of education in the former is dominantly formulated within the framework of an economic discourse. The latter points to education as a means to alleviate poverty, foster democracy and strengthen individuals and subordinated social groups (not least women) (cf. Robertson 2005). Although the three organisations all emphasise what education can do for the nations or countries (UNESCO), member states (EU) or economies (OECD), the OECD and the EU stress education as a prerequisite for economic progress, while UNESCO emphasises alleviating poverty, fostering democracy and empowering individuals and subordinated categories. The OECD and the EU thus dominantly constitute education in relation to an economic market, producing learners who can contribute to a growing economy, whereas UNESCO constitutes education as a human right and a tool for

Why education? 109

producing equality and democracy. The difference in emphasis is salient in how the OECD and the EU use the term 'growth' for the economic benefits of education, in contrast to UNESCO, which uses the term 'development'.

Education as an economic resource

In the documents, education is subordinate to the economy, and thereby made into a tool in the interests of global capitalism. The heading for the editorial of *Education at a Glance* reads 'Investing in people, skills and education for inclusive growth and jobs' (OECD 2012a, p. 13). This is repeated in ET2020, which is described as a subdocument to 'Europe 2020', the EU's strategy for 'smart, sustainable, and inclusive growth over the coming decade' (European Union 2009, p. 1). People, labelled 'human resources', are placed in juxtaposition with 'financial resources', and both forms of 'resources' are 'invested in', and because they are 'investments' the investors can expect 'returns' (OECD 2012a, p. 17). This is a reiteration of the human capital and knowledge economy theory, which expects great yields from investments in education (cf. Schuetze 2006) and which plugs an economic discourse into an education discourse. This entanglement and merging of two discourses fuses the boundaries between the two so that education emerges as a tool in the interest of the economy, instead of intrinsically valuable. The overarching rationale for the OECD is consequently constructed as monitoring and steering education through the PISA, PIAAC (the OECD Survey of Adult Skills) and TALIS (the Teaching and Learning International Survey) systems and global reports and evaluations of educational outcomes in order to produce human subjects that both serve and are served by the interests of a global economic market.

The economic benefits of education are, in *Education at a Glance*, not only or primarily constructed as benefits for 'the economies'. The document strongly stresses the economic benefits of education for individuals, thereby constructing learners predominantly motivated by individual economic desires. It states that those with longer education cope better in situations of economic recession. This argument is supported by unemployment figures. *Education at a Glance* presents figures that not only show that those with higher education are more likely to find jobs even in bad times, the jobs they get are also better paid:

> The gaps in earnings between people with higher education and those with lower levels of education not only remained substantial during the global recession, but grew even wider. In 2008, a man with higher education could expect to earn 58% more than his counterpart with no more than an upper secondary education, on average across OECD countries. By 2010, this premium increased to 67%. Similarly, in 2008, women with higher education had an average earnings premium of 54% compared to their upper secondary-educated peers. By 2010, this premium grew to 59%.
>
> (OECD 2012a, p. 13)

The quotation makes individual economic interests into a major argument for higher education. This is further stressed by dollar figures on the economic gains of a tertiary degree (OECD 2012a, p. 162). In addition to individual economic benefits, education is also claimed to bring about better health and a longer life expectancy (OECD 2012a, p. 202). The educated subject is thus constructed as rich, healthy and successful within the frame of a neoliberal discourse. The accounts of individual economic benefits are followed by renditions of how society benefits from the higher tax returns that the high earnings induce and a relation between high education and low demands for social welfare, which is an additional gain from the perspective of society. The constitution of learners as predominantly economic subjects and as resources for companies and the economy is consequently dominant and strong in this document, and so is the constitution of society as predominantly an economic institution or entity.

The OECD economy discourse of education is reiterated also in the ET2020. As mentioned earlier, the overall objective for a common strategy for education is to 'make Europe into a world-leading knowledge economy' (European Union 2009, p. 1). This emphasis on the economy becomes slightly mitigated when plugged into other values, such as 'the personal, social and professional fulfilment of all citizens' and '. . . democratic values, social cohesion, active citizenship, and intercultural dialogue' (European Union 2009, p. 2). The former of these objectives points to an intrinsic value of education, presenting it as valuable to individuals not only in economic terms. The latter objective constructs education as an asset for the nation state, in that it produces social cohesion, that is, it produces loyal and active citizens (cf. Biesta 2014b). The tension between economic and personal benefits is salient also in the formulations concerning lifelong learning. ET2020 states:

> The challenges posed by demographic change and the regular need to update and develop skills in line with changing economic and social circumstances call for a lifelong approach to learning and for education and training systems which are more responsive to change and more open to the wider world and . . . the establishment of more flexible learning pathways . . . enhancing people's employability and adaptability.
>
> (European Union 2009, p. 3)

These are formulations that constitute education as something that could produce subjects willing, in their own and society's interest, to learn new things, start over, move on and adapt. Although this could be seen as mainly in the interest of the market economy, the formulation 'enhancing people's employability' decentres the demand to being constantly ready to take on new and more education into an interest not only of the market but also of the individual. By shifting the focus from employers' interest in finding suitable employees to individuals' interest in finding jobs, the document contributes to the neoliberal economy production of a precarious labour force with no or insecure employment (Butler 2015). From this precarious situation emerges a desire for lifelong learning, not primarily as a possibility, but as a necessity. It is a reasoning based on presumptions that technological innovations, market fluctuations, recession and changes in the labour market are results of natural forces. The economy is

Why education? 111

thereby constituted as foundational, and the principles of market economy are naturalised.

A naturalisation of the entanglements of the taken for granted neoliberal discourse on economy and education

Karen Mundy claims that the economic discourse of the OECD documents on education is better described as 'a social and institutionally embedded liberalism' rather than as neoliberal (Mundy 1999, p. 28). She states that this discourse differs from the neoliberal education discourse in that there is no emphasis on market solutions to educational insufficiencies. Although I agree that the neo-liberal education discourse might not be explicit in the documents scrutinised in this chapter, it is implicitly taken for granted and thereby emerging as a self-evident motivation for education, or rather, for investments in education. Although the emphasis on education as intertwined with economy in the OECD and EU documents can be seen as a reiteration of a general capitalist market economy rather than a neoliberal ideology, there are formulations, not least in the OECD documents, indicating that the neoliberal educational reforms in some cases are promoted as self-evidently beneficial. This is true for the promotion of the PISA system as a means to assess quality in education, and also in some of the policy directions. *Education Today 2013* states: 'Develop skills for *effective school leadership* [my italics] and make it an attractive profession'; 'Increase *job differentiation* [my italics] between new and experienced teachers to improve *effectiveness*' [my italics]; 'Manage *school choice* [my italics] to avoid segregation and increased inequities'; '*Target low performance* [my italics] regardless of background' (OECD 2012b, pp. 12–13). By repeating expressions and notions common in the neoliberal education discourse, the neoliberal market governance principles are plugged into the education assemblage. Education is thereby constituted as encompassing neoliberal New Public Management traits such as audit governance, the stress on competition and excellence, school choice, differentiation and practises based on research and evidence.

Another important trait of neoliberal normativity is the emphasis on competition and differentiation as forces that generate quality. They constitute the engine for both individual and social development. This produces a paradox in the argumentation, especially in the OECD documents, which base the call for more tertiary education on higher earnings for those who have completed exams. The assertion that tertiary education will pay off for both individuals and society does not take into account that this effect is likely to decrease when more and more people get this education. As Hugh Lauder points out in his critique of human capital theory in higher education, this not only affects the benefits of education for the educated, but also the intrinsic value of higher education (Lauder 2015). This is partly addressed in *Education at a Glance*, which states that it is the overall wage dispersion that drives much of the returns for both the individual and the public sector, and that 'a compressed wage structure will typically generate lower returns to higher education' (OECD 2012a, p. 171). This evinces a contradiction in the argument for a general increase in tertiary

112 *Eva Reimers*

education. In order for the argument for increased earnings to work, there need to be big wage differences and limited access to higher education. These two preconditions are never explicitly stated or argued for, however. Instead, the document puts forward an increase in higher education as a means to economic benefits for both individuals and society in general. This demonstrates that although there are articulations that stress the need for more equity, the whole argument presumes, and thereby affirms, a society signified by considerable inequality and wage differences.

Social goals, education and politics

In the documents from the three organisations, there are simultaneous articulations of a discourse of education as a tool to achieve prosperity and economic growth and of education as a tool to enhance democracy and create social justice. These discourses plug into each other so that economic growth and democracy merge as tantamount to each other. For example, following the rendition of societal and economic benefits of tertiary degrees, the OECD document *Education at a Glance* moves on to non-monetary benefits such as longer life expectancy, increased voting rates and more supportive attitudes towards equal rights for ethnic minorities (OECD 2012a, p. 14). This evinces a line where democratic participation is defined and measured as voting rates and is plugged in with a discourse of tolerance. The possible challenge to the cohesion of a society that might be posed by subjects constructed as minorities or 'other' in relation to an imagined majority is here disarmed by the processes of tolerance. The other is designated to a position as 'accepted different' without disturbing norms that bring about the majority (cf. Reimers 2010). From this emerges a conception of learners in terms of socialisation, where citizenship is constituted by competences that foster social cohesion and loyalty to the political system of the nation state (Biesta 2014b). There are consequently few openings for constructions of learners as democratic political subjects, where plurality, dissensus and agonism are prerequisites for democracy (Biesta et al. 2014; Mouffe 2005). The subjectivity emerging from the documents thus becomes, just like education, subordinated to the economy which benefits from social stability.

Like education, social goals are subordinated to economic goals. *Education Today 2013* states: 'OECD analysis has shown that there need be no contradiction between equity and efficiency, and indeed has underlined how damaging to economic as well as social goals is the phenomenon of exclusion and widespread under-achievement' (OECD 2012b, p. 100). The quotation evinces how the plugging of social goals into economy constructs the subordination of the social as conditions for economic growth. The same happens in the arguments for investments in early childhood education: 'Strengthening equity in education is cost beneficial, and investing in early years yields high returns, since it makes it possible to reap the benefits and reinforce equity efforts made at subsequent education levels' (OECD 2012b, p. 101). Despite recognising marginalised categories, the emphasis in the EU and OECD documents is not on the rights and needs of these persons, but on the threat to social cohesion that marginalisation

Why education? 113

entails. Education, rather than economic redistribution, is constituted as a means to overcome marginalisation. This is evident in the following quotation:

> OECD analysis has shown that there need be no contradiction between equity and efficiency, and indeed has underlined how damaging to economic as well as social goals is the phenomenon of exclusion and widespread under-achievement.
>
> (OECD 2012b, p. 100)

It is consequently in the interest of the economy that social tensions and distress be avoided. Ambitions such as equal education for all are thereby constituted not primarily in terms of justice or human rights, but as important goals for the economy, and with no mention of politics. The conception of the subject in education, in this co-articulation of economy, education and social cohesion, emerges as subjects that do not give rise to social dissensus by their marginalised positions, but as subjects that adapt and are productive.

What can emerge from the normative materialisations of the documents is not only affected by what is articulated, but also by what is conspicuously absent from the documents. Neither the OECD nor the EU documents address aspects of education that are related to social circumstances and the politics of nations. Education as a means to increase individual life chances and induce 'social benefits' is, in *Education at a Glance*, constructed as isolated from social background and the life chances this entails (OECD 2012a, p. 202). In constituting the length and level of education as the sole determinant of wage level, life expectancy, willingness to vote and a general supportive attitude to society, relations between causes and effects are blurred. Considering the overwhelming evidence showing that sociological variables are by far more determinant for school achievements than instructional or educational variables (cf. Berliner 2012; Condor 2011; Rudolphi 2011), the claimed benefits of education could thus just as well be attributed to the social background of those who are most likely to receive a tertiary degree as to the degree in itself.

There is an apparent difference concerning how the OECD and the EU documents make connections between social variables and education and how UNESCO addresses educational deficits. UNESCO constitutes lack of education, in this case referring to literacy and primary education, in terms of poverty and gender, stating:

> But a number of obstacles, including poverty, still keep 67 million children of primary-school age out of school, 53 per cent of whom are girls and almost 43 per cent of whom are in sub-Saharan Africa. Enrolment rates are slowing and being eroded by dropout, particularly in countries affected by armed conflict where over 40 per cent of out-of-school children live. Gender disparities continue to hamper progress in education. Around 17 per cent of the world's adults – 793 million people, of whom two thirds are women – still lack basic literacy skills.
>
> (UNESCO 2011, p. 6)

114 *Eva Reimers*

In plugging in education achievements not into the neoliberal market economy, but into poverty and war, another story about education emerges. Learning outcomes are here not solely constituted as inducing economic benefits, but also as dependent on economic and political prerequisites. Peace, wealth, gender equality, political stability and social equality are constituted more as prerequisites for 'education for all' rather than as effects of 'education for all'. This is further enhanced by the two priorities that are presented in the document: Africa and gender. However, the neoliberal education discourse is also reiterated in the UNESCO document in accounts of projects where education is employed as a tool to combat poverty, achieve peace and acquire stability in the wake of disasters, where economic growth is the higher goal (see, e.g., UNESCO 2011, p. 14).

Ambiguous lines emerging from global multilateral education discourses

Important questions in relation to the theme of this book are how multilateral education discourses produce different conceptions of superior goals for education, and how this affects the emergence of different notions about who learners are and what they are imagined to become. I have therefore mapped norms and discourses in some documents on education from the EU, the OECD and UNESCO.

These three multilateral organisations spend considerable amounts of money on assessing, monitoring and, in the case of UNESCO, executing education. In this, they are not alone. There is a plethora of transnational companies and organisations investing in and instigating education measures and policies (cf. Ball 2012; Coxon and Munce 2008; King 2007; Robertson 2005; see also Martinsson, Chapter 3 in this book). This indicates that the entanglement of education and economy in the documents and work of UNESCO isn't specific to these organisations. From a critical perspective, and a perspective convinced of the possibility and necessity of education as a space where political subjectivity can emerge, the constitution of education as subordinated to economy, as a tool for neoliberal capitalism, becomes a problem. It is a disarming of education.

Inspired by the concept 'rhizoanalysis' (Masny 2013, p. 341), my ambition has been to read the documents together with each other and some theoretical concepts in order to explore what they – separately and together – could become and perform, not to assert what they mean. With the term 'becoming', I am referring to how the documents separately and together plug into each other, to other discourses, to places and to practises, thus producing conceptions of education, economy, subjectivity, society, democracy etc. This is a reading that resists stable categories in favour of mapping becomings, making it possible to discern how resistance and alternative conceptions of education emerge in and from connections in the education assemblage.

One example is how education and economy plug into a human rights discourse, which, although most salient in the UNESCO documents, is also discernible in the documents from the other two organisations. Although the plugging in of education with economy seems to restrict the becomings of education

Why education? 115

to economic progress, plugging in the term 'development' to the education-economic assemblage opens up for other becomings of a different kind, namely becomings where education is constructed as a tool to elevate people from a life in poverty. However, this is not unequivocal. The line emerging from the entanglement of education-economy-development might just as well subordinate development to the interests of the global neoliberal market economy, thus taking little account of injustices and the subaltern. Simultaneous reiterations of neoliberal market economy, education and human rights constitute a messy assemblage producing different lines concerning the aim and goal of education.

UNESCO is a large, multilateral organisation with an ambitious program to reach the goal of 'Education for all'. However, its programs are short of funding (see, e.g., Watson 1999), and one way to find money for education projects in developing countries is to cooperate with NGOs and donors from the private sector (Ball 2012; see also Martinsson, Chapter 3 in this book). This plugging in of education practises with economic interests stabilises the economic discourse, or with the nomenclature of Deleuze and Guattari (1988), it produces the economy as a molar line, making it difficult, but not impossible, for other lines to emerge. Education thus becomes an economic investment expected to give monetary returns.

However, my argument in this chapter is that although education in these documents is by and large subordinated to the economy, this is not unequivocal. The human rights discourse, the recognition that war, poverty, discrimination and social segregation are problems that need to be overcome, simultaneously produce another, quite different story than the one of economic growth, of what education is and can do. From this entanglement, a line of education as a means to reach equality, peace and democracy can emerge. This line is further stabilised when it is plugged into contexts and experiences of precarity (Butler 2015). This political or empowering flight line makes way for becomings of political subjects. Education is here not experienced, or made use of, as a tool to affirm a perceived cohesive society. Instead, it affirms lack of cohesion. It makes visible pluralities, conflicts and dissonances in the present and can produce visions of new and different becomings, visions about what life in interdependence with others might be.

The neoliberal education norm is dominant in the multilateral organisations, and its influence on education governance is in many countries more than considerable. Nonetheless, when this norm is articulated together with a human rights discourse, which becomes further enforced by lived experiences of precarity, poverty, marginalisation and injustices, other becomings than economic subjectivities are made possible. Political subjectivity can emerge in unpredictable and seminal ways and thereby instigate change. The dominance of the neoliberal education discourse is not total.

Notes

1   The research on which this chapter is based has been developed from the project 'Class in Neoliberal Education Discourses', funded by the Swedish Research Council (VR 2009–6173).

116 *Eva Reimers*

2 http://ec.europa.eu/education/, http://www.oecd.org/education/, http://en.unesco.org/themes/education-21st-century

References

Ball, S.J. (2012). *Global education inc.* New York: Routledge.

Ball, S.J. (2013). *Foucault, power and education.* New York: Routledge.

Bank, V. (2012). On OECD policies and the pitfalls in economy-driven education: The case of Germany. *Journal of Curriculum Studies* 44(2): 193–210.

Barad, K.M. (2007). *Meeting the universe halfway: Quantum physics and the entanglement of matter and meaning.* Durham and London: Duke University Press.

Berliner, D.C. (2012). Effects of inequality and poverty vs. teachers and schooling on America's youth. *Teachers College Records,* 16(1), Available at: http://www.tcrecord.org/content.asp?contentid=16889.

Berliner, D.C. (2015) The implications of understanding that PISA is simply another standardized test. Presentation at the symposium Education by the Number, Göteborg June 8 – June 9, 2015.

Biesta, G. (2010). *Good education in an age of measurement: Ethics, politics, democracy.* Boulder, CO: Paradigm Publishers.

Biesta, G. (2014a). *The beautiful risk of education.* London: Paradigm Publishers.

Biesta, G., (2014b). Learning in public places. Civic learning for the 21st century. In Biesta, G, De Bie, M. and Wildemeersch, D. (Eds.), *Civic learning, democratic citizenship and the public sphere* (pp. 1–11). Dordrecht: Springer.

Biesta, G, De Bie, M. and Wildemeersch, D. (2014b). *Civic learning, democratic citizenship and the public sphere.* Dordrecht: Springer.

Butler, J. (2015). *Notes toward a performative theory of assembly.* Cambridge, MA: Harvard University Press.

Chan, J. (2007). Between efficiency, capability and recognition: Competing epistemes in global governance reforms. *Comparative Education* 43(3): 359–376.

Condor, D.J. (2011). Egalitarianism and educational excellence: compatible goals for affluent societies? *Educational Researcher* 40(2): 47–55.

Coxon, E. and Munce, K. (2008). The global education agenda and the delivery of aid to Pacific education. *Comparative Education* 44(2): 147–165.

Deleuze, G. and Guattari, F. (1988). *A thousand plateaus: Capitalism and schizophrenia* [Mille plateaux]. London: Athlone Press.

European Union (2009). Council conclusions of 12 May 2009 on a strategic framework for European cooperation in education and training ('ET 2020'). *Official Journal of the European Union.* (2009/C 119/02).

Grek, S. (2009). Governing by numbers: The PISA 'effect' in Europe. *Journal of Education Policy* 24(1): 23–37.

Grek S., Lawn M., Lingard B., Ozgaa J., Rinne R., Segerholm C. and Simola H. (2015). National policy brokering and the construction of the European Education Space in England, Sweden, Finland and Scotland. *Comparative Education* 45(1): 5–21.

Gruber, K-H. (2006). The German 'PISA-shock': Some aspects of the extraordinary impact of the OECD's PISA study on the German education system. In Ertl, H. (Ed.), *Cross-national attraction in education: Accounts from England and Germany* (pp. 195–208). Oxford: Symposium Books.

Kamens, D.H. (2013). Globalization and the emergence of an audit culture: PISA and the search for 'best practices' and magic bullets. In Meyer, H.-D. and Benavot, A. (Eds.), *PISA, Power and policy: The emergence of global educational governance* (pp. 117–139). Oxford: Symposium Books.

King, K. (2007). Multilateral agencies in the construction of the global agenda on education. *Comparative Education* 43(3): 377–391.

Laclau, E. and Mouffe, C. (1985). *Hegemony & socialist strategy*. London: Verso.

Lauder, H. (2015). Human capital theory, the power of transnational companies and a political response in relation to education and economic development. *Compare* 45(3): 490–493.

Masny, D. (2013). Rhizoanalytic pathways in qualitative research. *Qualitative Inquiry* 19(5): 339–348.

Meyer, H. and Benavot, A. (2013). *PISA, power, and policy: The emergence of global educational governance*. Didcot, UK: Symposium Books.

Mouffe, C. (2005). *On the political*. London: Routledge.

Mundy, K. (1999). Educational multilateralism in a changing world order: UNESCO and the limits. *International Journal of Educational Development* 19(1): 27–52.

OECD (2012a). *Education at a Glance 2012: OECD Indicators*. Paris: OECD Publishing. Available at: http://dx.doi.org/10.1787/eag-2012-en.

OECD (2012b). *Education Today 2013: The OECD Perspective*. Paris: OECD Publishing. Available at: http://dx.doi.org/10.1787/edu_today-2013-en.

Pons, X. (2012). Going beyond the 'PISA shock' discourse: An analysis of the cognitive reception of PISA in six European countries, 2001–2008. *European Educational Research Journal* 11(2): 206–226.

Reimers, E. (2010). Homotolerance or queer-pedagogy? In Martinsson, L. and Reimers, E. (Eds.), *Norm-struggles: Sexualities in contentions* (pp. 14–28). Newcastle upon Tyne: Cambridge Scholars Publishing.

Robertson, S.L. (2005). Re-imagining and rescripting the future of education: Global knowledge economy discourses and the challenge to education systems. *Comparative Education* 41(2): 151–170.

Rudolphi, F. (2011). *Inequality in educational outcomes*. Swedish Institute for Social Research 86. Stockholms universitet.

Schuetze, H. G. (2006). International concepts and agendas of lifelong learning. *Compare: A Journal of Comparative Education* 36(3): 289–306.

Sjöberg, S. (2015). PISA and global educational governance: A critique of the project, its uses and implications. *Eurasia Journal of Mathematics, Science & Technology Education* 11(1): 111–127.

Takayama, K. (2008). The politics of international league tables: PISA in Japan's achievement crisis debate. *Comparative Education* 44(4): 387–407.

UNESCO (2011). *UNESCO and education*. Paris: UNESCO.

UNESCO (2013a). About us. Retrieved from http://www.unesco.org/new/en/unesco/about-us/who-we-are/introducing-unesco/

UNESCO (2013b). Partners. Retrieved from http://www.unesco.org/new/en/education/partners/

Watson, K. (1999). UNESCO'S vision for education in the twenty-first century: Where is the moral high ground? *International Journal of Educational Development* 19(1): 7–16.

8 Political subjectivity, political struggle and political education in times of precarisation

Eva Reimers and Lena Martinsson

We have written this chapter in a Europe experiencing at least a million asylum-seeking refugees within the continent and hundreds of thousands of people who are stopped at the European borders and treated as if they had no human rights. At the same time, political discourses and practises are moving in protectionist, nationalistic and racist directions, unprecedented since the inception of the Second World War. This dislocation of values also entails measures that threaten some of the fundamental traits of democracy. In Poland and Hungary, nationalistic governments undertake undemocratic measures such as limiting free press, free speech and equal rights. In other countries, such as France, Britain, Denmark, Norway and Sweden, right-wing nationalist and racist parties are growing quickly and gaining considerable political influence in the parliaments and governments. Simultaneously, the dominant public discourse in news, press and – not least – social media are becoming increasingly hostile towards refugees and migrants. One pertinent example from Sweden is how the notion of 'refugee crisis' has changed from originally referring to the crisis for those who have to take great risks in their escape from war and oppression to now referring to a presumed crisis for the Swedish welfare systems due to the large numbers of asylum seekers. This situation has affected our thinking around politics, political subjectivity and how education can make a difference. In working on this book, we have found that the chapters can provide deeper understanding of what is happening, and of the possible role for education. This chapter is therefore both a comment and a reflection on the situation in Europe.

Residents in many countries face a situation where it becomes increasingly difficult to identify with the politics of states or the EU. When citizens in the different countries find their lives disrupted and social institutions unreliable or non-existent, it is not only the constructed character of nations and communities that becomes evident, it is simultaneously a situation which questions current politics. From this emerges political activity in differing directions and in different spaces. There has emerged a plethora of activities based in different sectors of civil society, such as churches, mosques, the union, women's movements, peace organisations, the Red Cross, some leftist organisations and so forth, putting pressure on governments to implement human rights and offer possibilities for refugees to seek asylum. They have mobilised for legal ways into Europe so that people don't have to remain in gigantic refugee camps or die on the

Mediterranean Sea. As recounted above, the situation has also contributed to the emergence of nationalist and racist right-wing activists, who present themselves as guardians of essential national identities and values.

The main questions for this book are neoliberal reiterations in education and how political subjectivity can emerge, that is, a subjectivity that not only recognises that there is a need for social change, but also carries an understanding of being able to contribute to that change. The above points to the need to recognise that the actual content of political subjectivity must be democratic if we believe in a society where human rights are recognised. In order for political subjectivity to be democratic, it needs to acknowledge inequalities, power relations and the fundamental situation of interdependence. At present, it is not only war, poverty and terrorism that subvert the possibilities to recognise these values and recognise the inevitability of interdependence. The neoliberal stress on the rational, independent individual who is supposed to make choices based on her/ his own interest also undermines notions of human rights, human interdependence and inter-responsibility (cf. Brown 2015). For us, interested in the role of education, we ask what this misrecognition of human interdependence means for the possibility of education, and for the emergence of political subjectivity. What can this politically unstable situation, where social cohesion is put under pressure, tell us about the conditions required for political subjectivity to emerge?

On the messy situation in Europe and emergences of political subjectivities

In early September 2015, the image of the dead body of a three-year-old refugee boy named Alan Kurdi, washed ashore on a beach in Turkey, was spread in news and social media all over the world. The small inflatable boat in which the family had tried to go from Turkey to Greece had capsized, and lacking proper a life vest, the boy drowned. Although there had previously been images of thousands of drowned refugees, images that the European people seemed to get used to, the image of the dead child on the shore gave rise to strong reactions all over Europe. It became impossible to continue ignoring the fact that people are dying due not only to war but also because of European immigration politics, sometimes likened to building 'fortress Europe'. However, after some months the reaction subsided, but at the same time, it became more and more obvious that there were strong tensions and struggles about what Europe was going to be.

The realisation that people were dying at the borders led to different reactions among people living in Europe. Social media was filled with outrage over inhumane immigration politics, and during the autumn of 2015, huge demonstrations were organised all over Europe. These demonstrations were roughly of two categories. One welcomed refugees and opposed strict border policies. The other claimed that the influx of people would change and even destroy Europe and the European nation states, and therefore opposed open border policies. The latter category of demonstrations was not a new phenomenon. For example, the anti-Muslim organisation Pegida had regularly gathered in Dresden against immigration of Muslims to Europe since the autumn of 2014, and later also in other cities.

120   *Eva Reimers and Lena Martinsson*

Criticism of Europe's restrictive immigration politics was, of course, not new either. However, during the autumn of 2015, it became more apparent, stronger and more transnational. Coordinated demonstrations in different countries and cities, as well as the emergence of large social media networks, changed the dominant discourse from fear of the scale of asylum seekers to a stress on the human demand to help people in need. The insight into how European politics had contributed to the deaths and terrible situations for refugees prompted huge groups of people to go to the streets and demand change. This process was closely connected to the role of social media. People reacting and gathering in the cyber-world made it possible for large numbers of people to form new alliances, constituting political communities, claiming a reality that is not yet materialised in official politics (Butler 2015). Even if we find the assemblies of material bodies to be of extreme importance for the growing democratic struggle, we also want to address the importance of social media as part of this assembling force.

Protests and resistance against restrictive European immigration policies didn't suddenly appear in the autumn of 2015. They were there already. For us and many others, the already problematic identity as European, with Europe's history of colonialism and exploitation and interventions in the Middle East, has made it even more difficult to identify with the European project. For others, it was a wake-up call. In any of these cases, we, as protesters, disidentified with both EU and individual nation state politics. As activists, we came together to demand change, to work for a different Europe. But the gathering of thousands of bodies articulating similar criticisms made not only the lack of cohesion and the plurality within Europe visible, it also made it obvious that there were other sorts of possible collectives and imagined belongings, another possible 'we' than those emerging from a notion of the nation state. This disidentification with present politics at the same time acknowledges past and current European atrocities as something to learn from. Divisions of people's rights and values based on ethnicity, race and religion have, in the history of Europe, always ended in disaster. The big demonstrations and the huge social media network can be seen as performative events, staging and making real the hope of creating another future Europe. In assembling in big numbers, a new 'we', a new collective, signified by a shared disidentification with the state apparatus as well as strong dissociation from nationalist movements, appeared in the public. Bodies gathered together in action are powerful in calling into question reigning notions of the political (Butler 2015). A collective political subject was constituted and held together by the relations in the assemblies of bodies in different places.

The other category of assemblies of bodies in discord with European and national migration politics, the nationalistic right-wing movements, can also be seen as political subjects dissociating from reigning politics. In their gatherings, a quite different alternative to the current EU immigration politics was constituted. Where the protesters above based their critique on the democratic values of freedom, equality and solidarity, or human rights, the nationalist critique of European policies is based on differentiation and exclusion of people due to citizenship, ethnicity, race and religion. When the nationalists participate in official politics, their definition of democracy is limited to the notion of elections and

Political subjectivity 121

majority rule. They are not recognising the preconditions for democracy, such as respect for equal values between human beings. The inadequate conception of democracy as a form, reiterated in the neoliberal market discourse, as well as by the nationalist movement is also, according to Gert Biesta in Chapter 2 in this book, often repeated in the school's citizenship education. The entitlement to freedom and equality is restricted to imagined communities of individuals who are represented as having a stronger claim to these rights than those who are positioned outside. Because the nationalist movements don't recognise or abide by the fundamental democratic principles, they cannot be recognised as a valid option in a democracy (Mouffe 2005).

It is important to note that the assemblies who want to stop refugees from entering the European nations, even if they identify themselves as nationalistic, also work in a transnational arena. They are part of a transnational movement. To give an example, the name of the German nationalist and anti-Muslim movement, Pegida (Patriotic Europeans Against the Islamisation of the Occident) addresses the whole imagined European community. People gather in protests under the name Pegida in many European countries. The Pegida movement thereby constructs an imagination of a cohesive, white and Christian Europe, a movement beyond the nations and national identities but in strong opposition to an idea of what they themselves denominate 'multiculturalism'. There are populist racist parties in all European countries, and they have many collaborators and connections. If social media have been and continue to be of great importance for the movement for a more open Europe, this is even more the case for the racist nationalist movement. Besides meeting face to face in conferences and congresses, they use social media to recruit followers, establish networks and arrange anti-immigration rallies and activities. Chantal Mouffe points out the importance of antagonism and agonism for the political to emerge and become passionate (2000). She has, in many texts, warned about how a politics striving for consensus makes democracy impossible. She claims that this type politics produces extremist parties, wanting something else, positioning themselves outside the struggle for consensus. Europe today shows that she was right in her predictions. There is today a very strong antagonism, a strong constitutive border between 'us' and 'them' that is impossible to ignore as it is expressed in gatherings in public squares and in large rallies and manifestations. The extremist parties are not only in public squares, but also in parliaments and governments. However, in social media, there are few meetings between opponents, between 'us' and 'them', and the racist nationalist movements, as well as the movement for an open Europe, have found spaces in social media where it is possible to develop their own agenda without being interrupted or questioned, a situation that precludes meetings between different positions as well as the agonism that Mouffe puts forward as the core of democracy.

The above points to the importance of differentiating between political subjectivity and political democratic subjectivity. Both movements described enact political subjectivity in relation to the imagined cohesive Europe. However, it is only the movement for an open Europe where all humans are met and recognised as individuals with equal rights that can be identified as democratic. An important

122 *Eva Reimers and Lena Martinsson*

point we want to make is that there are two opposing alternative understandings of what Europe could or ought to be. Where the movement for a more open EU aims for more or 'better' democracy (Biesta et al., Chapter 2 in this book), the nationalists work towards an undemocratic Europe. In this, both movements partake in the ongoing construction of the imagination of Europe.

The struggle for democracy and human rights is not only a struggle between the two movements. There are also other fronts, other lines of conflict where the question of democratic rights is central. Although the short history of the EU of today is full of tensions and conflicts concerning policies, procedures, relations between nation states and relations between the EU and individual nations, there have also always been many tensions between the states and the EU in relation to civil society in Europe. There is, for example, a struggle about the economy and the unequal economic order between the nation states. These tensions, together with the refugee situation, are also producing transnational movements such as the Democracy in Europe Movement (DiEM25) launched in Berlin in February 2016, stating that the European Union will have to be democratised or disintegrate, and they also stress that they 'refuse to retreat into their nation states' (DiEM 2016).

The present refugee situation in Europe has made it evident that the EU and the European nations openly override the human rights and democratic values they usually claim to uphold. At the same time as democratic values are reiterated by extensive parts of the civil society and by activists, the EU as well as some of the member states, such as Sweden and Hungary, oppose human rights and democratic values by denying refugees the right to seek asylum. In Europe and the US, among other regions, the question of human rights has long been individualised. A person has rights that could be violated through, for example, discrimination. However, what can be discerned in Europe is that the rights to rights – the right to live, and live livable lives (cf. Butler 2004), the right to seek asylum, the right for families to reunite, the children's convention – are no longer a common ground. These values have today become a political question that must be understood as strongly antagonistic. It has become a struggle beyond the realms of democracy.

Education and political subjectivity

Fundamental values such as equal rights and democracy are threatened and even overridden in Europe today. In situations like this, education becomes a target for a subversive politics, democratic as well as undemocratic. Education is a tool for nation states, as well as multilateral organisations such as the OECD, UNESCO and the EU, to shape the young in order to make way for a desired future. In this way, education is saturated by politics and aimed at constructing a cohesive nation state, although the character of the nation is constantly subjected to debate and changes. Curricula and school policies are outcomes of political debates and decisions about the role of education for the nation and the individual pupils. As Foss Lindblad and Lindblad show in this book, the notion of the educated, who they are and who they need to become, is contingent and changes over time and place. Foss Lindblad and Lindblad recount that in Sweden, the comprehensive school with the goal of preparing citizens to enact an equal society has now been replaced, or at least complemented, by the goal of preparing students to become consumers and flexible lifelong learners in a neoliberal economy. We think it is important to try to grasp the huge risk for the struggle for democratic values and democratic organisations, that this individualisation, the notion that one is responsible only for oneself, and a diminished understanding of human interdependence, entails. The strong neoliberal ideal of today is undermining human rights, because human rights need to be respected and enacted. Human rights need communities. Below, we will recount three examples of norm struggles in education that could make way for the emergence of democratic political subjectivity (cf. Martinsson and Reimers 2010).

Curricula struggles

The position of compulsory education as a tool to reach political goals makes education into a space for political struggle. Whoever has power over education also has power over the future of the nation, or at least over which norms should be decisive in shaping the future. In Sweden, in the autumn of 2014, the political aspect of education became salient in relation to migration and national identity. The nationalist and racist party Sweden Democrats (Sverigedemokraterna) presented a motion in the parliament proposing changes in the national preschool curriculum (Motion 2014/2015:2937). The changes they proposed reflected their political goal of reconstructing what they understood as 'Swedish culture' and 'Swedish cultural heritage' from a notion of a multicultural nation to a monocultural nation. The proposed changes targeted three areas: cultural heritage, gender and language. The suggestion was to replace the educational goal of multiculturalism with the goal of fostering 'the Swedish cultural heritage'. The ambition to actually foster the Swedish cultural heritage was different from how the Sweden Democrats understood the role of education for gender equality. In the bill, they proposed to change the goal to 'counteract traditional gender roles' to one stating that 'boys and girls' should have 'rights and possibilities' to 'test and develop abilities and interests without unwarrantable influence from adults'. Thus, when it came to gender, there was no need for education to intervene as there was regarding cultural heritage. The party reiterated a common trait among nationalist parties, which is to disrecognise feminist movements and initiatives to achieve gender equality and LGBTQI rights. In relation to language, the motion recognises only two possible national identities within the nation: Swedish or one of the recognised national minority languages. All children with other mother tongues fell outside these positions: their only option was thus to adopt the Swedish cultural heritage and the Swedish language. The preschool was constituted as a space for construction of a homogeneous Swedish nation, where children with backgrounds from other countries should be assimilated into a presumed Swedish culture. A limited conception of what the Swedish can contain would be enforced. The idea of a monocultural Sweden should thereby be materialised. The bill was met with great resistance

124   *Eva Reimers and Lena Martinsson*

from other political parties as well as from educational scholars and teachers, and it was eventually turned down.

Clandestine children and the struggle between children's rights and immigration legislation

The critique raised against the bill from the Sweden Democrats demonstrates again that education is a place for political struggle, not least in terms of who the educated are supposed to be and become. Before 2013, the right for all children to go to school did not include clandestine asylum seekers, children without documents, living unofficially in Sweden and often hidden (Sager 2011). The decision to give these children the right to schooling can to a certain extent be understood in line with the neoliberal educational discourse, which stresses the right to education for all individuals so they can develop their potential and contribute to the country's economic growth. However, granting these children the right to education evinced a conflict between the human right to education and the immigration laws which denied clandestine families asylum and citizenship. Having the children in school positions them inside society, while at the same time, the families are considered illegal and face deportation. The paradoxical conflict is a performative: it creates a tension that can challenge both the human rights and the immigration policy. Teachers with clandestine children in their classes thereby find themselves in a political situation which disrupts the notion of political and social cohesion. In relation to schooling, the children are part of Swedish society; they are children in Sweden. In relation to their families, they are positioned outside society. In having these clandestine children in class, the position of the children as inhabitants of Sweden is enacted and confirmed. The position of the teacher becomes a political position of tension where it is obvious that something in the practises and notions of habitation, citizenship and nationality is wrong. It becomes impossible for the teachers to easily put their trust in a hegemonic order because this order is challenged. It is possible to understand this situation as 'values schizophrenia', as Jos Harvey and Jessica Ringrose do in their chapter. We see this stressful messiness not only as a problem, but as a situation where a possible political subjectivity of the teachers can emerge. Something is wrong, and teaching becomes a way of doing difference, of doing Sweden differently. Another Sweden can be performed, a Sweden in which these children partake. The presence of the children in the classroom can thereby transform the idea of society. The paradoxical situation, experienced by the teachers and also by the exposed children and their families who are simultaneously part of the Swedish society and excluded from it, is one where possible political and democratic subjectivity can emerge.

Unaccompanied children, racism and school as possibility for the emergence of another society

Another example of placing refugee children inside and outside at the same time is the situation that has emerged for many of the refugee children coming

Political subjectivity 125

without parents, the so-called unaccompanied children. The situations for these children have become increasingly difficult. In order to follow what at the time was understood as a democratic principle, many municipalities arranged information meetings for inhabitants when new homes for care and residency (hem för vård eller boende, hereafter HVB) for these children were planned. We attended six of these meetings and followed, through the media, what happened at similar meetings in other cities. We soon started to realise that many of these meetings, but not all, became places for people to express cultural racist views, that is, stereotypical, depreciating and excluding views about certain groups or religions (Mulinari and Neergaard 2014). The opponents of the HVBs received support and applause for their racist opinions. In this way, a racist and nationalist space was enacted, a racist culture emerged. At three of the meetings we attended, the children were talked about as dangerous, and at one, meeting demands were raised to keep guards around the HVB in order to protect the neighbours. Parents repeated cultural racist 'worries' about Muslim people and connected Islam to sexual violence and rape. The questions repeatedly asked concerned the safety of their own children. Could they ever go to the beach again without being sexually harassed or even raped? We also observed how the moderator of one of the meetings, as well as the politicians and staff from the municipality, lost control and the meeting became a space for fascist and racist mobilisations. It became a very significant moment for right extremist political subjectivity to emerge in the name of 'our' children – meaning white, Christian, Swedish children. These meetings were obviously not democratic. The principle of all humans being of equal value was of no importance. Some children were valued more than others; 'our children' were contrasted to 'them'. The idea of taking care of others was questioned. The understanding of interdependence beyond one's own narrow, white, Christian group was abandoned. Diana Mulinari and Anders Neergaard write about arguments like these as 'racism of care'. An example is how the Sweden Democrats claim that people who 'care' for others, where the other is limited to those who are considered as belonging to the same community (in terms of race or culture), cannot really be racist, they are just caring. They argue that they are acting responsibly for those who are already part of the Swedish nation and culture, stating the need to first of all 'take care of our own' (Mulinari and Neergaard 2014). This discourse of caring can also be discerned in other parts of Europe, such as the Netherlands, where the right-wing Party for Freedom claims, when they want to prevent Muslims from receiving asylum in their country, that they are taking care of the interests of homosexuals in the country so they will not be subjected to homophobia (cf. Puar 2007).

At one of these meetings, a teacher stood up and talked from quite another perspective, opening up for other possible ways of thinking. The teacher became an important political subject, reminding those of us sitting in the room about democratic principles as well as the professionalism of the work done in schools. He, and he was also soon supported by the school's principal, told us about how the school had at first been somewhat worried when they learned that 14 unaccompanied children were about to enrol. Their worries were unfounded. The boys were smoothly integrated into the school. The teacher's and principal's

126 *Eva Reimers and Lena Martinsson*

experiences and how the boys participated with their new schoolmates made another sort of vision possible. The boys became part of a school and thereby part of Sweden.

As in the example with clandestine children, the situation demonstrated that the school was, and can become, a place where a larger and changeable 'we' emerges. But there is always a risk that the school could be a place for assimilation, where children need to leave their own cultural heritage in order to fully adhere to what are presumed to be Swedish values and culture. The political struggle is not only going on between different groups of people. It is also going on within individuals. At another meeting some weeks later, the same principal underlined, after first expressing again how ambitious and well behaved these boys were, the importance of educating the children in 'Swedish values and culture'. She expressed that this was even more important than teaching them Swedish. Thus, in less than two minutes, she reiterated both a discourse where she recognised the boys as ambitious and fine individuals, and a discourse that could have been pronounced by the Sweden Democrats with their demands for assimilation of those who intend to stay in Sweden. The principal thereby didn't recognise the boys' own cultures, identities and emergences, believing instead that they should learn something defined as fixed Swedish values. This shows how racist norms can be and are repeated in many different contexts, and by people in different positions.

These many struggles, literally over people's lives, make schools into extreme political and antagonistic places. Not as a function of implementing the political curricula, but as a place for direct political struggle. As we are writing this, we don't know what will happen. The struggle over which society we shall have and whose lives are going to be possible to live is ongoing. It is possible, however, to see that schools can be spaces where a different and more open notion of society is enacted and made real.

Plurality and the emergence of political subjectivity in the classroom

Different norms and normative materialities in education produce contradictory interpellations (Mouffe 2013). It becomes possible to understand the society, the school, oneself and others in many different ways. In this plurality, we find possibilities for democratic political subjectivity as well as risks for non-democratic subjectivity to emerge. A central concept and present condition in this process is plurality. With plurality we do not – and this is very important – mean a plurality of an assembly of presumed essential identities, such as homosexuals, men, people of colour or people from different classes. We see, in line with Butler, an insufficiency of identitarian ontology (Butler 2015). These understandings of identities do not embrace the importance of the ongoing production of both differences and interdependence. The emergence of the 'I', as an experience and conception, takes place within an entanglement of norms, practises and other 'I's'. Existence in itself is relational. To be a person is to be dependent on recognition from and relations to other humans as well as non-humans. It is to be dependent, to live in interdependence. When we talk about plurality in relation

Political subjectivity 127

to education, we allude to this multitude of interconnections. We understand plurality and interdependence as prerequisites for political subjectivity. Plurality is therefore not something that needs to be overcome in schools and everyday life in order to establish a coherent space; quite the contrary. What is needed is a recognition of, what we have previously named 'disharmonious pluralism' (Martinsson and Reimers 2008). The struggle for a coherent space can be oppressive, not recognising different lives as livable. Instead, plurality needs to be acknowledged as a possibility. The ongoing production of pluralities needs to be constantly scrutinised and made salient, as well as used and embraced in schools and education. This can be compared to Takayama's suggestion in Chapter 5, using the nationalistic conception of Japan as a subject for studies in history and social science in order to develop new ways of making sense of the image of Japan and what it means to be Japanese. The school, as a place of contradictions, of human encounters, of bodily assemblies, makes it possible to imagine other societies, other and new ways of constructing the social. It is consequently possible or even necessary to decentre the school in the European situation today, from the governance of PISA and other neoliberal governance practises to a space for political imaginations and enactments of a plural society.

As Biesta states in Chapter 2 in this book, citizenship in education is rarely formed in relation to plurality. The most prevalent conception of citizenship in citizenship education in schools is social citizenship, that is, teachings aiming at producing citizens that are loyal to and uphold and maintain the political institutions and who thereby contribute to social cohesion. The same conception of citizenship informs the documents on education from multilateral organisations, analysed by Reimers in Chapter 7. Democratic participation is here limited to voting and other forms of contribution to social cohesion, which in turn is subordinated to the economy. This means that plurality and difference, just like in the nationalist discourses accounted for above, are mainly perceived as problems that needs to be overcome.

Another way to maintain cohesion, prevalent in education, is the discourse of tolerance. This is a discourse that both presumes and produces a perceived other that must be tolerated (Brown 2008, Reimers 2010). This discourse of tolerance is prevalent in citizenship education that stresses social cohesion. Tolerance means that the normative majority from a privileged position identifies and positions some categories as 'other', assigning them to subject positions that are tolerable but with no significance for the majority. They are included but do not belong. Instead of challenging dominant norms and recognising plurality, this strategy stabilises the idea of a cohesive society and the positions of the dominant majority. This simultaneously positions 'the other' outside of what is seen as the norm and gives those who are tolerating the benefit of feeling generous. Tolerance is thus a power practise where those understood as the other are subordinated to an imagined 'we'.

A third strategy used to handle plurality and difference within citizenship education informed by social cohesion is democracy as deliberative communication (Englund 2006). Tomas Englund proposes deliberative communication as a strategy or principle for education that will contribute to forming citizens that can participate in the deliberations that he sees as the core of democracy. It is a notion of pedagogy and democracy based on Habermas's conception of communication as a means to form consensus. A prerequisite for this perspective is that although individuals are different in many ways, it is possible to construct spaces for communication where each voice has the same value, and by communicating respectfully and with the aim of reaching a common good, consensus can be reached. In stressing the possibility and goal of overcoming dissensus, the strategy of deliberative communication repeats and asserts the notion that it is important to construct and maintain social cohesion, thereby denying the ubiquitous presence of a plethora of contesting and conflicting norms, and ensuing positions and interests. Citizenship education in the form of deliberative education risks obfuscating hierarchisation and oppression that emerges through materialisations and articulations of the plurality of norms. In using the notion of equal and rational human subjects as a presumption, the strategy does not take into account the constructedness and fluidity of different subject positions.

We believe that in order to open up for a democracy that can counteract today's burgeoning nationalism and racism, it is important to create awareness about how schooling and education can be a space for political subjectivity. Or to say it another way, to create awareness about how schools can be spaces where political subjectivity can emerge and more porous conceptions of society can be enacted.

The conflictual situation where Europe fails to live up to what is meant to be its standards produces frictions that could be an important condition for retellings on a European level. Europe is an imagined community and has been constructed as such through contrasting itself in relation to other continents. Many of these continents have been understood as different and inferior. Europe has constituted itself as Christian as well as secular, as the origin of democracy and as the most modern and democratic of continents (Asad 2013; Said 1978). Following Takayama, it is important to find new reference points, or find new perspectives in the reconstructive process, not only in schools, but in society as a whole. We believe that in order to actually try to construct a better democracy that can work in a world with people on the move over the continents, it is necessary to develop a transcontinental construction, where Europe understood as an independent unit is challenged and its interdependency with other parts of the world is made part of its self-understanding. The presence of refugees in Europe can hereby be seen not as outsiders wanting to come in, but as assemblies of bodies enacting their right to appearance in Europe as equals. An understanding like this might be a way to be responsible and a way to narrow the divide between the European 'we' and 'the others'.

References

Asad, T. (2013). Free speech, blasphemy, and secular criticism. In T. Asad, W. Brown, J. Butler and S. Mahmood (Eds.), *Is critique secular? Blasphemy, injury, and free speech* (pp. 20–63). Berkeley: UC Berkeley Townsend Center for the Humanities.

Brown, W. (2008). *Regulating aversion: Tolerance in the age of identity and empire*. Princeton, NJ: Princeton University Press.

Brown, W. (2015). *Undoing the demos: Neoliberalism stealth revolution*. New York: Zone Books.

Political subjectivity   129

Butler, J. (2004). *Undoing gender.* New York: Routledge.

Butler, J. (2015). *Notes toward a performative theory of assembling.* London: Harvard University Press.

DiEM (2016). *Diem 25.* Accessed online, 1 March 2016. Available at: http://diem25.org/

Englund, T. (2006). Deliberative communication: A pragmatist proposal. *Journal of Curriculum Studies* 38(5): 503–520.

Martinsson, L. and Reimers, E. (2008). Towards a disharmonious pluralism: Discourse analysis of official discourses on social diversity. In A.M.Y. Lin (Ed.), *Problematizing identity. Everyday struggles in language, culture, and education* (pp. 51–65). Milton Park and Abingdon: Lawrence Erlbaum Ass.

Martinsson, L. and Reimers, E. (2010). *Norm-struggles. Sexualities in contentions.* Newcastle Upon Tyne: Cambridge Scholars Publishing.

Motion 2014/15:2937. *Ändringar i Lpfö98 (reviderad 2010).* [Changes in the preschool curriculum 98 (revised 2010)]. https://www.riksdagen.se/sv/Dokument-Lagar/Forslag/Motioner/ndringar-i-Lpfo-98-reviderad_H2022937/?text=true.

Mouffe, C. (2000). Politics and passions: The stakes of democracy. *Ethical Perspectives* 7(2–3): 146–150.

Mouffe, C. (2005). *On the political.* Abingdon and New York: Routledge.

Mouffe, C. (2013). Hegemony and new political subjects. In J. Martin (Ed.) *Chantal Mouffe: hegemony, radical democracy and the political* (pp. 45–57). London: Routledge.

Mulinari, D. and Nergaard. A. (2014). We are Sweden Democrats because we care for others: Exploring racisms in the Swedish extreme right. *European Journal of Women's Studies* 21(1): 43–56.

Puar, J.K. (2007). *Terrorist assemblages. Homonationalism in queer times.* Durham and London: Duke University Press.

Reimers, E. (2010). Homotolerance or queer pedagogy? In L. Martinsson and E. Reimers (Eds.), *Norm-struggles. Sexualities in Contentions* (pp. 14–28). Newcastle Upon Tyne: Cambridge Scholars Publishing.

Sager, M. (2011). Everyday clandestinity: Experiences on the margins of citizenship and migration policies. Diss. Lund: Lunds universitet.

Said, E. (1978). *Orientalism.* New York: Pantheon Books.

9 Political subjectivity and the experiment of democracy: a conclusion

Lena Martinsson and Eva Reimers

In this concluding chapter, we will discuss the outcomes of the book and tie the main threads of the arguments and analyses together. All of the chapters are informed by the notion that schools can be transformative political spaces. Despite neoliberal normativity in education, the book shows that within dominant neoliberal educational governance, where neoliberal normativity makes politics and political subjectivity superfluous and where achievement tests and audit culture delimit educational practises (Harvey and Ringrose, Foss Lindblad and Lindblad, and Reimers in this book), there is still room for the emergence of political subjectivity. The education assemblage encompasses contradictory norms and practises that plug into each other in multiple and not totally foreseeable ways. Besides the neoliberal emphasis on measurable knowledge, the education assemblage includes citizenship studies, human rights and critical thinking. Consequently, the chapters make way for a critical discussion about the multiple emergences of global and local materialisations of educational norms as well as about how political subjectivities are made (im)possible. By drawing on the arguments from the chapters, we want to contribute to a theoretical discussion of neoliberal norms in education, pointing to the messiness and the situatedness of their materialisations, and to the unpredictability of what can and will emerge within and alongside educational practises.

There are three outcomes of the chapters that we especially want to emphasise in this summary. The first is the potential emergence of political subjectivities even in a neoliberal context. Second, closely connected to this, is the importance of different forms of plurality for political subjectivity and democracy to emerge. The third important outcome addresses 'the experiment of democracy' and its transformative role in educational spheres and for educational practises. Together, these three outcomes advocate an anti-nostalgic way of understanding the role of society and education in the wake of neoliberalism.

Political subjectivity and the need for pluralism

As many of the chapters show, neoliberalism harbours a depoliticising performativity, which is an effect of its emphasis on market-economy logic as the foundation for society and the solution for societal problems. The subordination, and in some cases even invisibilisation, of politics in favour of the economy is pointed

A conclusion   131

out by Foss Lindblad and Lindblad as well as Reimers. In their chapters, they all describe neoliberalism in education as a form of governance, which limits constructions of education and the educated as well as practises and teachings pertaining to civic education. Foss Lindblad and Lindblad map governance in education and take as their point of departure a media event where the economic transnational organisation OECD was made the main advisor on Swedish education reforms and policies. They relate this to how the goal of education in terms of the expected subjectivity of the learner has been constructed in different Swedish national curricula. Their mapping evinces a gradual transformation of 'the educated' individual as an informed citizen aligned with the interest of the nation-state into a flexible learner and consumer serving the interest of the (global as well as national) economic market. Important to note is that different rationalities on the significance of education do not simply replace each other; they coexist, producing tensions and making way for partly contradictory perceptions of possible subjectivities, political, economic, or both. In her analysis of policy documents from the transnational organisations EU, OECD and UNESCO, Reimers points to entanglements of education and economy which subordinate education to the economy, so that getting an education becomes equated with an investment in the interest of monetary prosperity. Although this is salient in all the documents, in the UNESCO documents, the main motivation for educating people draws from normativities pertaining to human rights. Education is thus constituted as essentially good and a right for everybody. This entanglement of education with both human rights and neoliberal market norms makes way for political subjectivities wherein individuals act not in the interests of themselves and the market, but in the interests of larger collectives and the society as a whole.

In the neoliberal- and New Public Management-informed educational practises, education tends to be limited to measurable and predefined outcomes, leaving little room for political subjectivity to emerge. This is the point of departure for Harvey and Ringrose, writing about the creation of a neoliberal equalities policy in a primary school in London. The creation of this policy was a requirement under the Education Act 2010, and the idea was to formulate accountability by developing measurable outcomes, preferably related to test results amongst different groups. In following this work, Harvey and Ringrose noted how the focus on measureable outcomes based on gender, race and income obfuscated children's experiences of inequality, and at the same time the process formed spaces where these experiences could be articulated and recognised. In line with Biesta's assertion in Chapter 2, this shows that children are fully capable of acting politically. Consequently, becoming political is not necessarily a matter of socialisation from 'above'.

While acknowledging the neoliberal effects of constructing consensus and depoliticising societies, the chapters in the book contribute to a more complex and paradoxical understanding of neoliberalism in education. One important concept for taking issue with neoliberalism in education is political subjectivity, which we understand as constituted by three dimensions. These are: a sense that (1) something in the present situation is wrong, (2) there are alternatives to this situation and (3) I or we can bring about difference. The book highlights the role

132   *Lena Martinsson and Eva Reimers*

and significance of plurality as present and significant for the emergence of political subjectivity in educational practises and situations dominated by neoliberalism. Several chapters in the book assert that interpellations as political subjects, despite the dominance of neoliberalism, are made possible by simultaneous articulations of contradictory norms, making it difficult to predict what the entanglements of differing normativities will produce. This connects to Mouffe, who is an important thinker for most of the authors. In line with her thinking, plurality and agonism are regarded as preconditions for democracy and the political (Mouffe 2005). Mouffe not only addresses the importance of different contradictory normative interpellations for political subjectivity to emerge (Mouffe 2013), she also stresses the importance of a plurality of ways to imagine alternative societies (2005). In this book, Biesta, in line with Mouffe, stresses the importance of not seeing plurality (of identities, discourses, positions, subjectivities and opinions) as an obstacle that has to be overcome in order to form cohesive societies, but rather as the actual condition for the emergence of democratic citizenship, which in his thinking comes very close to political subjectivity.

In her analysis of policy documents on education from different transnational organisations, Reimers shows how plugging different neoliberal market discourses into discourses of human rights and education makes way for different conceptions of the aim of education. Analysing the education policies in terms of assemblages of a plurality of norms makes evident how they produce differing possibilities for the emergence of political subjectivity, sometimes together with and other times contrary to the dominant market economy norms. Likewise, in line with Mouffe, Martinsson focuses on the importance of a plurality of norms and materialities for political subjectivities and the political to emerge. In the rural Pakistani village that Martinsson studies, neoliberal normativity becomes one of many normative forces. Together, these forces cause contradictory interpellations, creating a situation where it can be obvious that life and society can be understood and organised in different ways. Plurality of norms and positions is salient in Chapter 8 also. The focus here is on Europe as it faces a million asylum-seeking refugees. Reimers and Martinsson recount how different political subjectivities emerge in situations that can be understood in many different ways. This can result in the emergence of antagonistic positions, not least between those who advocate welcoming refugees based on humanity and human rights on the one hand and those who advocate closed borders based on nationalistic and protectionist values on the other hand. Reimers and Martinsson assert that these antagonistic norms are also salient in the Swedish classroom, where teachers and pupils simultaneously experience both restrictive immigrant policies and human rights discourses. Teachers with clandestine children in their classes find themselves in a situation which disrupts the notion of political and social cohesion. The children become part of the Swedish society due to their rights to schooling. However, as members of undocumented immigrant families, they are positioned outside society. Vulnerable children, their families and the teachers are all interpellated in contradictory ways, forming ambiguous, vulnerable and precarious situations for the pupils and the families. The situation is antagonistic and should not be normalised, but instead severely challenged. At the same

A *conclusion* 133

time, it is a situation where possible political subjectivity, democratic as well as undemocratic, can emerge.

The experiment of democracy

Although recognising how education is entangled with norms that delimit what is possible to do within education in relation to the possible emergence of political subjectivity, this book takes a positive and hopeful position regarding the possibilities of education as a transformative force. In this section we will use the term 'the experiment of democracy' to show how this can be practised in educational spaces.

Biesta introduces 'the experiment of democracy' as a way of describing what signifies democracy and suggesting what could signify educational practises that aim for political subjectivity. The idea is that democracy is always under construction. It is not primarily a matter of opening up for including more subjects or positions, or of constructing more democracy; rather, it is a continuous process of transformation forming a better democracy.

When Takayama suggests engaging with and reconstructing nationalism in Japan, this can be understood as an experiment of democracy. He suggests that, rather than refuting or silencing Japanese nationalism, it could be reconstructed as something that can be practised by pupils and teachers in their classrooms. This, Takayama claims, can make it possible to understand how constructed and problematic the dominant understanding of the nation is and to make new imaginaries of the Japanese society, culture and citizens. In this way, a problematic nationalism aiming for homogeneity rather than plurality can be subverted, and a more open and plural image of Japan as a transformative place can emerge.

A second suggestion for how to work with a possible democratic experiment in education is to bring the messiness of norms and materialities into the classroom. Instead of trying to produce an image of a cohesive society, it is possible to focus on the many norms and discourses that reproduce but also can be part of transforming society as well as identities. In the Pakistani village featured in Martinsson's chapter, the different norms and ideas about how to organise society made it obvious that the village was a place for possible transformations. The neoliberal, socialist and feudal norms made it possible to imagine that the village could change. There were contradictory interpellations. To talk about and learn to recognise this messiness as something that has potential is a democratic experiment in learning about the conditions of contingence and the possibilities for politics. But it is also important to notice the democratic experiment performed by the pupils. The schoolchildren were attributed a role of transformative actors when they were told to persuade the parents who weren't letting their children attend school to change their minds. It was possible even for children who were working to become pupils in school. It was possible for individuals to reconfigure identities, to change, to become someone else.

A third example that can inspire democratic experiments when exposed to neoliberal audit practises is the work of the pupils in the chapter by Harvey and Ringrose. The Office for Standards in Education, Children's Services and Skills

(OFSTED) demanded that the school formulate an equality policy based on what could be measured in achievement tests relating to gender, class and race. When the pupils were interpellated and recognised as subjects with knowledge, they analysed the situation in school in a complex way. The pupils' practises of democratic thinking opened up possible transformations of the school; their own experience became valued and understood as making change for all. The recognition of the pupils' own analyses can open for a way to practise democracy. They, as well as the children in the Pakistani village, learned from what Biesta might have identified as 'current citizenship', and they were talked to and recognised as citizens or political subjects. Through the practises the pupils took part in a democratic experiment, an open, never-ending transformative work.

Even if we are hopeful about the possible emergence of political democratic subjectivities, that is, subjects who want to change the present in the direction of a better democracy, we also recognise that these processes and transformations encompass and produce distress and discomfort. Furthermore, the experiment(s) of democracy are ongoing. They are processes without an end, they give rise to questions without answers, and all democratic performances are provisional. However, the book shows that neoliberalism is always performed together with a plurality of norms. This produces possibilities not only for segregation, marginalisation and hierarchisation, but also for transformations in the direction of more plural and open democracies.

References

Mouffe, C. (2005). *On the political.* New York: Routledge.
Mouffe, C. (2013). Hegemony and new political subjects. In J. Martin (Ed.), *Chantal MouffeHegemony, radical democracy and the political* (pp. 45–57). London: Routledge.

Index

Abe, Shinzō 75
accountability 49, 50–1
achievement goals 10
active citizenship 15, 102
agency 2, 19, 21
Alm, Erika 32
Althusser, Louis 75
Anderson, Benedict 75
Archard, David 77
Arendt, Hannah 20, 21, 30
'Asia as method' 82–3
assemblages 7–8, 11, 32, 39, 46, 102–5

Baacha Khan Trust Educational
    Foundation (BKTEF) 35, 36
'bad nationalism' 77
Baker, D. 51
Ball, Stephen 50
Bauman, Zygmunt 24
Benavot, Aaron 103
Berlin Wall 68
Biesta, Gert 2, 5, 6–7, 8–9, 14–30, 38,
    45, 75, 79, 105, 121, 127, 132
Bologna Process 106
Bonded Labour Liberation Front
    Society (BLLFS) 35, 36, 40, 41
Butler, Judith 21

Calhoun, Craig 76, 77, 79, 80
Cameron, David 49
Chen, Kuan Hsing 68–9, 83
children: capacity of living together in
    plurality 30; clandestine children 7,
    124, 126, 132; in Pakistan 43–5;
    rights 124; unaccompanied children
    124–6; vulnerable children 132
choice 29, 72
Churchill, Winston 16
citizenship: democratic education and
    78; discourses on 21; as political

identity 23; political subjectivity and
    2–3; social and political conceptions
    of 14–17; social cohesion and
    3, 14–15; as socialisation 3; as
    subjectivisation 3
citizenship education 2, 7, 21, 29, 87,
    127–8
civic education 19, 77
civic learning 23, 25, 29, 30
civic nationalism 76–7, 81
civil learning 45
clandestine children 7, 124, 126, 132
cohesion 2–3, 5–6, 127
Cold War 68
'cold-war-era education scholarship' 70,
    72, 74
collective decision-making 25
collective identity 9, 76
collective interest 28
'common schools' 78, 80–1
Communist Party 70
competition 4, 5, 10, 49, 51–2, 93
compulsory education 2, 10
consensus 17, 39
constitutional patriotism 77
contradictory interpellation 41, 43, 45,
    46, 126, 132, 133
corporate social responsibility (CSR) 37
cosmopolitan education 78
cosmopolitanism 77
Critical Race Theory (CRT) 62, 64
Crombie, A.C. 94
CSR Pakistan 37–8
culture 77, 80
'current citizenship' 134
curricula struggles 123–4

Dahlberg, G. 51
decentralisation 10
Decline of the Public (Marquand) 27

136 *Index*

'de-cold-war' politics 69
deliberative communication 127–8
democracy: as 'conflictual consensus'
   17; definitions of 16; as deliberative
   communication 127–8; desire for
   27; experiment of 22–30, 133–4;
   nationalism, education and 75–80;
   as a particular historical invention
   16; as process of transformation 24;
   as staging of dissensus 17–19; as
   thoroughly political project 16–17;
   values of 16, 17
Democracy in Europe Movement
   (DiEM25) 122
democratic agency 19
democratic citizens 90
democratic citizenship 30
democratic education 78
democratic participation 2, 127
democratic politics 21
'democratic subjectivity' 21
democratisation 18–19
denationalisation 103
deregulated school markets 10
Derrida, Jacques 20
desires 26, 28
development goals 102
difference 15
differentialisation 2
discrimination 5–6
disidentification 19, 27
dissensus 17–19, 20
diversity 6
'diversity management' 6
Dudley-Marling, C. 51

Eastern Europe 75
economic colonisation 103
economic discourse 11
economic relationships 29
education: changing discourses on
   89–93; compulsory education 2;
   critiques of education available to
   subaltern children and children from
   the lower classes 33–4; dominant
   economic discourse and 11; economic
   and political subjectivities in public
   discourses on 101–15; as economic
   resource 109–11; and/as economy
   107–12; educational interventions
   34–7; entanglements of the taken
   for granted neoliberal discourse on
   economy and 111–12; experiment
   of democracy and 22–30, 133–4;
   human rights and 11, 102; as

investment and/or human right
   108–9; marketisation of 2, 37–9;
   marketised reforms 9, 10; nationalism,
   democracy and 75–80; neoliberal
   interventions 37–9; neoliberalism
   and 1–2; as on the one hand practises
   and on the other hand politics 105;
   as part of state apparatus 75; plurality
   and emergence of political subjectivity
   in classroom 126–8; as political
   project 87–9; political subjectivity
   and 122–6; politics of state regulation
   of 88; role of education for national
   sentiment 77; social goals and politics
   112–14; as tool for prosperity and
   better future 11; use of national
   sentiments in 9
Education Act 50
educational assemblages 7–8, 10,
   39–45, 102–5, 130
educational discourses 7
educational recommendations 96–7
educational reforms 2, 7, 9
educational systems 87
Education and Training 2020 102, 107
Education at a Glance 102, 108, 109,
   111, 112
education governance: changing
   discourses on 89–93; decentralisation
   10, 90; globalisation 91, 93;
   marketisation 10, 90–1, 93; by
   numbers 10; reformation 10, 90
Education Today 111, 112
Ekta Parishad 34
English school system 9
Englund, T. 87, 127
Equalities Act 49, 58
equality 11, 17, 18, 57–8
equality objectives 9
equality outcomes 61–3
ethnic markers 74, 80
ethnic nationalism 76, 80, 81
ethnocentric genocide 75
European Union (EU): ambiguous lines
   emerging from global multilateral
   education discourses 114–15;
   Bologna Process 106; education and/
   as economy 107–12; *Education and
   Training 2020* 102, 107; education
   as an economic resource 109–11;
   education as investment and/
   or human right 108–9; education
   assemblage 10, 102–5; education
   as tool for 122; education in
   documents 106; entanglements of

the taken for granted neoliberal
discourse on economy and 111–12,
131; immigration policies 119–20;
reiterations and reterritorialisations of
concepts and ideas 107–8
evaluations 7, 93, 109
exam results 54–7
exclusion 22
'external conditioning for education' 71
extremist parties 121

Feinberg, Walter 77, 80
female entrepreneurship 38
feminist movements 36
feudal mindset 39–41
Foss Lindblad, Rita 10, 103, 104, 131
Foucault, Michel 10
freedom 16, 50, 72, 76, 105, 120
free school choice 10
Fundamental Law of Education (FLE)
70, 72–4, 80

Gandhi, Mohandas K. 26
'gap discourse' 58
gender equality 64, 123
gender issues 58–9, 64
Gillborn, D. 51
global citizenship 21
global multilateral education discourses
114–15
Gramsci, Antonio 33
Great Britain: equality objectives in
primary school 49–65, 131; exam
results 54–7; neoliberal traits in 4;
quantification of equalities issues
53–4
Gutmann, Amy 78

Habermas, Jürgen 77, 128
Hacking, I. 94
Harvey, David 39
Harvey, Jos 5, 9, 131, 133
hegemony 2, 7, 11, 20, 22, 42–3, 69,
103
Hiopak 37
Hirohito, Emperor of Japan 69
Hirota, Teruyuki 72, 74, 79, 80
homes for care and residency (hem för
vård eller boende [HVB]) 125
Honneth, Axel 22
human atrocities 75
human relationships 28
human rights 11, 108–9
Human Rights Commission Pakistan
(HRCP) 36

Hussain, Khadim 33, 34, 35, 36, 45
Hussain, Neelham 33–4, 36, 45

identification 19
identity 14, 18–27, 32, 44; collective
identity 76; cultural identity 80;
democratic identity 21; national
identity 73–4, 77–82, 123; political
identities 21, 76–7; problematic
identity 120
identity markers 74, 80
identity politics 26, 29, 77
identity position 6
imagined community 75, 76
immigration legislation 124
immigration policies 119–20
Imperial Japan 75
Imperial Rescript 70, 71
inclusion 22
India 34
inequality 5–6, 18
interdependence 11, 42, 46, 105, 115,
119, 123, 125–7
International Association for
the Evaluation of Educational
Achievement 106
interruption 6, 8, 18
interventions: educational 34–7;
neoliberal 37–9
Irie, Yōko 74

Japan: 'cold-war-era education
scholarship' 70–1; cold-war spell
69–72; depoliticisation of education
70–2; educational reforms 5;
enacting de-cold-war politics 80–3;
Fundamental Law of Education 70,
72–4, 80, 81; 'love of country' 72–4,
79, 83; nationalism, democracy and
education 75–80, 133; neoliberal
traits in 4; school assessment criteria
81; textbook screening 70; use of
nationalism in education 9–10; US
Occupation Regime 69–70; US
strategic interest in 68–9
Japan Teachers' Union 70, 71

Kang, Sang-jung 75
Kayano, Toshihito 75
Kennedy, John F. 15
Khan, Nighat 36
Kodama, Shigeo 75
Komikawa, Kōichirō 74
Korea 68
Kuhn, T.S. 94

138   *Index*

Kurdi, Alan 119
Kymlicka, Will 76, 82

Lahore College for Women University 32
learning 23–5, 29, 35, 43, 133
Learning Democracy in School and Society (Biesta) 14
Liberal Democratic Party (LDP) 69–71, 72
liberal polity 77
liberty 17
life-long learner 88
life-long learning 108, 110
Lincoln, Abraham 16
Lindblad, Sverker 10, 103, 104, 131
'love of country' 72–4, 79, 83

Maguire, M. 64
Mahmood, Saba 44
Mandela, Nelson 26
Marquand, David 27, 29
Martinsson, Lena 4, 7, 9, 11, 132
Maruyama, Masao 75
master-slave dialectic 22
meritocracy 60–1
Meyer, Heinz-Dieter 103
Miller, David 75
Mills, C. Wright 24
Ministry of Education (MoE) 70–1, 72
molar lines 7
Morita, Naoto 71
Moss, P. 51
Mouffe, Chantal 3, 16–17, 20, 24, 39, 46, 78, 121, 132
Mundy, Karen 111
municipal schools 10
Muslims 119

National Agency for Education 91
national belonging 77–8
national bonding 75
national identity 15, 73, 74, 77, 79, 80, 82
nationalism 7, 9–10, 75–80, 133
nationalistic values 15
nationalist movements 11, 121–2
national sentiment 75–6, 80
'national tradition' 81
Nazi Germany 75
neoliberalism: democracy and 28–30; education and 1–2; nationalism and 7; neoliberal interventions 37–9;

neoliberal normativity 3–4, 5–6; political subjectivity and 131–2
neutrality of education 71, 82–3
non-governmental organizations (NGOs) 33, 40–2, 115
norms: in assemblages 7–8; neoliberal 3–4, 5–6; plurality of 7
Nussbaum, Martha 78

Office for Standards in Education (OFSTED) 9, 51, 60, 133–4
Okinawa 68, 69
Organisation for Economic Co-operation and Development (OECD): ambiguous lines emerging from global multilateral education discourses 114–15; analysing premises of OECD evidence as a style of reasoning 94–6; education and/as economy 107–12; education as an economic resource 109–11; education as investment and/or human right 108–9; education assemblage 10, 102–5; education as tool for 122; *Education at a Glance* 102, 107, 108, 109, 111, 112, 113; education in documents 106–7; *Education Today* 107, 111, 112; entanglements of the taken for granted neoliberal discourse on economy and 111–12, 131; expanding statistical evidence into educational recommendations 96–7; Programme for International Student Assessment 56, 93–4, 95, 102, 103–4, 106, 111; Progress in International Reading Literacy Study 106; reiterations and reterritorialisations of concepts and ideas 107–8; report on education in Sweden 86–7; Trends in International Mathematics and Science Study 103, 106; at work in educational settings 93–7
Ōuchi, Hirokazu 74

Pakistan: corporate social responsibility in 37–8; educational interventions 34–7; feminist movements 36; feudal mindset 39–41; messiness 39–45; neoliberal interventions 37–9; neoliberal traits in 4; one child, many positions 43–5; school system 31–2; women become political subjects 41–3

Index

Patriotic Europeans Against the Islamisation of the Occident (Pegida) 119, 121
patriotism 77
peoplehood 77, 79, 80
performative measures 9
performativity 49, 52–3
plurality 6–8, 15, 26, 45–6, 132
police order 17, 19, 22
political action 22
political agency 2, 23–4
political democratic subjectivity 121
political identity 21–3, 76
political institutions 20–1
political language 76
political neutrality 72
political relationships 29
political socialisation 87
political subjectification 2
political subjectivity: education and 122–6; emerging in pluralities 6–8; formation of 2–3; individual conception of 19–22; in messy assemblage of Pakistan 39–45; messy situation in Europe and emergences of 119–22; and the need for pluralism 130–3; opposing forms of 11; plurality and emergence of in classroom 126–8; political democratic subjectivity and 121–2; within political institutions 20–1; use of national sentiments in education to form 9
political values 17
politics 18, 87–9, 112–14
Politics of Piety (Mahmood) 44
power 20, 22
precarisation 5–6, 45, 118
precarity 115
private schools 10
Programme for Individual Student Assessment (PISA) 91
Programme for International Student Assessment (PISA) 56, 93–4, 95, 103–4, 106, 111
Progress in International Reading Literacy Study 106
public domain 27–8
public place 27–8
public services 29
public sphere 27, 29, 77

race 57, 59–60
race/ethnicity-based identity politics 77

racism 124–6
Rancière, Jacques 6, 17–20, 22, 24, 79
rational deliberation 77
reasoning 94–6
recognition 21–2, 36, 80, 115, 126–7, 134
refugee children 124
refugees 11, 119–21, 132
Reimers, Eva 6, 11, 127, 132
relative autonomy 75
religion 59–60
repetition 4, 19
research case study: creation of equalities policy 53–65; equality outcomes 61–3; exam results 54–7; gender issues 58–9; meritocracy 60–1; quantification of equalities issues 53–4; race/religion 59–60; views on equality 57–8
res publica 24
'rich-poor' pupil gap 56
Ringrose, Jessica 5, 9, 131, 133

school assessment criteria 81
school performance 92–3
school quality 10
schools: function to develop national sentiment 77–8; as place for experiment of democracy 25–6; as spaces for political struggle 11
scientific paradigms 94
segregation 2, 6
self-interest 28
Siddiqui, Shahid 33, 34, 45
Simorgh 33–4, 36, 41
social cohesion 3, 14–15, 102, 127
social goals 112–14
socialisation: citizenship as 3; conception of civic learning 6, 23, 29, 30
Socialist Party 70
social order 17–18
social relations 75
society 15
'soft governance' 87
Spaces of Global Capitalism (Harvey) 39
Spivak, Gayatri Chakravorty 9, 33, 34, 45
standardised solutions 10
statistical evidence 96–7
student subjectivity 79
subjectification 6, 19, 23, 27, 75, 81
subjectivity 20–1, 32
Sweden: corporate social responsibility in 37; curricula struggles 123–4;

140 *Index*

education governance 10, 89–93, 132; governance of compulsory education 86–98; nationalist and racist party education reforms 123–4; neoliberal traits in 4; OECD report on education 86–7, 93–7
Sweden Democrats (Sverigedemokraterna) 123

Tahara, Hiroto 70
Taiwan 68
Takayama, Keita 5, 7, 9, 46, 133
Takeuchi, Yoshimi 83
Thatcher, Margaret 15
'the educated' 87, 88–9
'the people's right to education' 71
tolerance 112, 127
Torney-Purta, J. 87
transnational movements 121–2
Trends in International Mathematics and Science Study (TIMSS) 103, 106
'triage system' example 51

unaccompanied children 124–6
United Nations Educational, Scientific and Cultural Organization (UNESCO): ambiguous lines emerging from global multilateral education discourses 114–15; education and/as economy 107–12; education as an economic resource 109–11; education as investment and/or human right 108–9; education assemblage 10, 102–5; education as tool for 122; education in documents 106; entanglements of the taken for granted neoliberal discourse on economy and 111–12, 131; reiterations and reterritorialisations of concepts and ideas 107–8; *UNESCO and Education* 102
United States (US): Occupation Regime in Japan 5, 69–70; strategic interest in Asis 68–9

values 15–16, 17; basic 91; democratic 104–5, 120, 122–3; dislocation of 118; educational 92; equal values 121; fundamental 122; moral 72–3; national 8, 78; Swedish 126
value schizophrenia, 52–3
Viroli, Maurizio 77
vulnerable children 132

welfare state 36
White, John 77, 82
women: empowering 36; female entrepreneurship 38; as political subjects 41–3; voting rights 18–19

Youdell, D. 51
Yousafzai, Malala 1

Zia-ul-Haq, Muhammad 36